WINDMILLS TO SUBMARINES

MEMORIES OF A SMALL-TOWN TEXAS KID
1938 – 1958

RICHARD WITTE, PHD

This book is dedicated to kids of all ages and the value of play.

Go outside and play. Play with your cousins. Play with your friends. Play with folks who have different backgrounds. This is America, our diversity is our strength.

Play basketball. Play volleyball. Play in the band. Play football. Sing in the choir. Run track. Work on the school newspaper, Play baseball. Play softball. Play soccer. Work with a local charity. Be involved. Be a team player. Life is a team sport. Compete and give it your best and that will always be good enough.

MY STORY

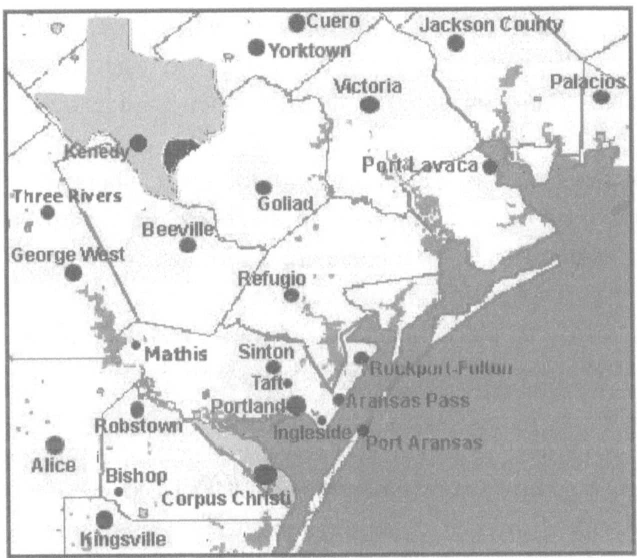

This map shows the area of my world as a kid. In my world, I was free to play. I was free to screw up. Everyone I knew was a surrogate parent. Every day my mom said, "Go outside and play and have a good time. If you get into trouble, I will know about it. Be careful with that BB gun. You could shoot an eye out. Don't be late for supper."

This book is based on vivid and treasured memories of being a kid in small towns in South Texas. I was an outside kid. If I was inside, I was in school or it was time to eat, sleep, study or I was grounded. Everything in this book will be true to those memories.

I will never forget Shorty, my fighting gamecock with a disability. Shorty had one leg shorter than the other. Shorty never acknowledged his disability, and he challenged his archenemy, my dad, every day. I cannot remember where the final battle occurred, so I have used imagination and storytelling to share this family tragedy.

To protect the innocent, and challenges to my memory, I have only used real names where I am sure those involved would not mind their names being used.

All Catholic Nuns mentioned in this story are *Saints*. I've not used real names for the *Saints* in this story. Thank you, Sisters.

My experiences with multiple characters have consolidated in my memory. As I visited colleges in the late 1950s, I was impressed with the Korean War veterans attending college on their GI Bill. I have consolidated their input into a single person I named Leonard. Leonard is a real person to me. I value his guidance on my life decisions. Leonard was real, but he was not a single person.

Characters with speaking parts in this book are real and true to my memory. Some of these characters are no longer available to speak for themselves so I speak for them. I cannot let the story of folks like PW Morrow with his paint speckled white shirt, tie and Stetson hat disappear. Their stories should provide inspiration and smiles to future generations.

Where memory is clear, but facts are not, I use imagination and storytelling to convey my true memory.

You decide if my story is true enough to be a memoir.

Dick Witte

CONTENTS

1

BEEVILLE TEXAS

1938-1943

PW Morrow, Maternal Grandfather (Grandad)

"Don't touch that boy! I told him he could climb that windmill. It's my windmill."

Good afternoon. My name is Preston William Morrow, but my friends call me PW. My grandkids call me Grandad and that is my favorite name. I know some in the family call me other names that I don't appreciate, but that's their problem.

With me it's 'what you see is what you get'. I often wear the Irish label as a small businessman. I'm a painting contractor. My boys, Billy and Gene, had been doing most of the painting while I drummed up new business. Then they went off to war.

I'm painting again, to keep a roof over our heads. I will be sixty years old soon and, for someone who has lived my life, sixty is old for those damned extension ladders.

As far as I know, only Irish blood flows in my veins, as befits the name, Morrow. I'm an American by birth, and a Texan by choice. My Great-Granddaughter Sarah will discover we're American back to Samuel Barrett, who fought in the American Revolution.

I'm just a Baptist Irish American hillbilly who is damn glad to be out of the hills and into the scrub of South Texas. I'm not sure why it took us so long to get here, but I love Texas. I guess I got here as quick as I could. We, as a family, migrated out of Appalachia down through Arkansas and Louisiana and finally to South Texas.

We are small-town Texans. I think we are a bit different from the cowboys and the big city Texans, but we are all in agreement that we love Texas. Across America, the small businesses and their workers are the backbone of America. America always gets the job done. Guys like my sons left their work and will go overseas and they will win this war. We work hard; we take care of our families, we usually go to church, we serve our country when called and we try to help those who need a hand or a handout. I will stay here in Beeville, Texas with my family, the chickens, the cows, and all the rest on East Milam Street until my time is finished.

Since my boys left for the war, I am both a painter and a businessman. I wear a starched white shirt with strategic paint speckles and a tie under my overalls. I keep my Stetson hat, a Silver Bellied Rancher, in the car. I can slip off my overalls, put on my hat, and be ready to make a professional painting estimate in a matter of minutes. These are tough times and we need to be ready for every opportunity to do business.

Today I'm doing a favor for one of my grandkids, the newest grandkid. Dickie is a good boy, but I'm afraid that he is headed for trouble. He has broken the rule about not climbing the windmill more than once. I will always support him. That sometimes gets us both into trouble.

Just last week, he climbed my windmill again and was just sitting there surveying the world when I came by to load paint. I said, "You know if your mom catches you, you'll get a switching." Dickie knows I don't care if he climbs the damned windmill. Those women let the kids climb that Live Oak tree in the front yard and swing from ropes. More than one kid has lost a tooth or two on a bad landing. That old oak tree is taller than my windmill, but those women put my windmill off-limits. I think it's because they don't have any rocking chairs to sit in to watch the windmill. They had rather sit on the front porch, rock, watch the tree and the kids, and gab. Sure enough, last week, just as Dickie was climbing down from the windmill, his mom came by with a salt cedar switch in her hand.

I saved his little ass, but it made for bad words between me and his mom. I don't like to have words with my kids, but this time it was a good excuse to quit work and head for the tavern. Dickie loves to go to the tavern and eat pretzels, drink root beer and hold my Stetson. Last week, after the latest windmill incident, he stayed home with his mom. I'll take him with me on my next painting estimate. He can hold my hat while I go in the house. If I get the job, then we will go to the tavern. If I get into the house, I usually get the job. The ladies appreciate a man who bothers to wear a white shirt and tie and takes his hat off to come into their house. It is just a matter of respect. I always give a fair price and my sons have demonstrated the quality you get with a Morrow paint job.

Dickie has the unfortunate last name of WITTE, which is a German name. German names are not popular these days. Dickie's name is not his fault. The truth is he looks more Irish than German to me. He looks and acts just like my son Gene.

Herbert, Nannie Lee and Windmill

Today I'm supposed to introduce myself. I'm proud to be one of the main characters in Dickie's life in Beeville.

Dickie lives across the street from my house. He calls it the Grand Old House. He spends every spare minute at my house playing with his cousins, Ruth, and Patricia, and it is where I get him out of trouble with his mom, Nannie Lee. His Mom is a true Irish lass and a real beauty. My wife, Ruth Morrow, says we did well with Nannie Lee. I upset Ruth and Nannie Lee, on occasion, like the windmill incident, but we're family. We forgive everything and we move on. There is work to be done and life to live.

As World War II grew to include America, our mostly happy family, and my business, was disrupted. My sons went off to war. My sons were my workers in our family business. My son Gene went to Pearl Harbor as a sailor and my son Billy went to Europe to fight the Nazis. Dickie's dad accepted a draft deferment and moved his family from Beeville to an oil refinery in the little town of Ingleside, Texas. The workers in my business were gone, and the person I called on to fix mechanical problems moved to Ingleside.

Dickie loved his life in Beeville before the war disrupted our family. Dickie probably did not understand that - even in this time of war - our family was fortunate. The Great Depression had just been declared over, but the scars of that time lived with us. However, we're all employed. We have enough to eat. Even one of the ladies in our family is working.

Alene, my son Gene's wife, is a professional secretary. I know that many ladies in the family admire Alene for swimming against the tide. I just admire her for her practicality. She has skills and she uses them for the family.

I am glad that Dickie's dad, Herbert, didn't go overseas. Herbert is still close enough for me to call on when I need help. That man is a genius with things mechanical. As a house painter, I'm more of an artist than a mechanic.

Dickie and his Granny will also introduce themselves and will give you their story of the time when Dickie lived across the street from me. I am not sure how he got Granny Ruth to talk. I have been married to her for a long time and I seldom get her to talk to me other than to say "no" or "you didn't fix the fence." On a good day she might say, "PW, you look good today, go to work and be good." It will be interesting to see what she has to say.

PW Morrow and Granny

Granny, Grandad, and Cousins: Pete, Dickie, Ruth,
Patricia and Juanita - 1940

DICKIE'S BEEVILLE STORY

"Where's the milk?"
"Where's the action?"
"I am tired of being cooped up!"

I came into the world kicking and screaming, according to Mom. I was born at the Beeville, Texas Hospital at 7:15 a.m. I was awake early as is still my way. I got here in time for Christmas of 1938. I spent most of Christmas at Granny and Grandad's house and received two bibs and a rattle. I was ready for food and could make some noise. Mom's Baby Book said I weighed 8 pounds, 8 ounces, and was 19½ inches long at birth. It also said I arrived looking for my next meal. Hunger has remained an enduring trait. I think the 'kicking and screaming' was just my need for a little excitement.

Dr. Reagan delivered me and removed my tonsils a few years later. No matter where we lived in South Texas until I was a teenager, he was our doctor. Dr. Reagan was the only doctor I saw until I was turned over to Dr. Auten in Ingleside for my freshman football physical. We didn't go to a doctor's office often in those days. The first dentist that ever examined my teeth was in Navy Boot Camp in San Diego, California in 1957. Mom always said I had great teeth and the Navy dentist agreed.

Nannie Lee and Dickie

Mom, Nannie Lee, was pretty and kind. I was sure that I had the best and most beautiful Mom in the world. Mom, like her mom, understood 'Unconditional Love' before Carl Rogers coined the phrase. They were big fans of Jesus, who made love the focus of the new covenant about two thousand years before Mr. Rogers. Mom and

Granny always had a reading from Saint Paul's First Letter to the Corinthians posted in their houses:

A reading from the first Letter of Saint Paul to the Corinthians

Love is patient, love is kind. It is not jealous, is not pompous, it is not inflated, it is not rude, it does not seek its own interests, it is not quick-tempered, it does not brood over injury, it does not rejoice over wrongdoing but rejoices with the truth. It bears all things, believes all things, hopes all things, endures all things. Love never fails. The word of the Lord.

Dad was the epitome of the hard-working blue-collar man. He had been active in sports at Cuero High School in Cuero, Texas. Dad also played a year of baseball after high school. He turned down a scholarship offer to Texas Tech University. Dad said it was a football scholarship. My Aunt Marie later showed me his scholarship letter and I noticed it did not say anything about football. I am sure Dad had a high IQ. I believe that his scholarship offer had something to do with his academic ability. His father was an academic, an engineer, and an inventor who went broke in the Depression. I'm sure that Dad believed that college was a waste of time. Herbert Witte believed that everyone learned best by doing.

By the time I was born, Herbert was four years out of high school. He had already progressed from driving a wrecker to journeyman mechanic for trucks, heavy equipment, and automobiles. He would soon be in high demand for his skills. If it was mechanical, Dad could fix it or, if necessary, build it. He once built a four-cylinder Indian motorcycle from scrap parts.

When Herbert and Nannie Lee took me home from the hospital, it was to East Milam Street in Beeville, Texas. I lived across the street from Granny and Grandad Morrow and my Uncle Billy, Aunt Sue Ellen and cousins, Ruth, and Patricia. We were all one family. Ruth and Patricia (respectively two years and one year older than me) were like sisters. Even though she and I do not see each other often,

Patricia, the only other survivor of that Beeville family, is still a sister to me.

My Uncle Billy was a role model for my entire life. Aunt Sue Ellen was one of my two lifelong spiritual advisors. My Beeville family also included Uncle Gene, PW's other son, and another lifelong role model. My Uncle Gene was one reason I chose the U.S. Navy as my first working career. Gene's wife, Alene, was the first and only lady I knew who worked outside the home. I admired her, and I know Mom did too. Then there were my cousins Juanita and Pete, who lived out in the country. Their mom, Hilma, was Mom's older sister. Pete and I were buddies and had many great adventures a few years later, although I did not see his family much during my first five years.

Dad's family lived close enough for me to see and bond with while we lived in Beeville. Grandpa Witte, Grandma Witte, and my Aunt Marie lived in Cuero, Texas. Dad said Cuero was about 'two flat tires' away from Beeville.

My Aunt Norma, Dad's other sister, her husband Edwin, and my cousins Bernard, Bobby and Francis lived in Victoria Texas, about 30 miles from Cuero.

Grandpa's brothers and sisters lived mostly in Central Texas. Our branch of the Witte family began in the community of Frelsburg, in Colorado County, Texas, which was

Herbert and Dickie

settled in 1837 by immigrants from Germany. My great grandparents wed and settled in Frelsburg after they emigrated from different parts of Germany. Grandpa's family was active in Central Texas.

The Witte side of the family, and my Boldt cousins in Victoria, did not show much overt affection. They were hand shakers, strong hand shakers, while the Morrow side of the family in Beeville, were huggers. My Victoria cousins were a bit older than me, so we were not quite as close as my Beeville cousins. They were the essence of small-town blue-collar Texans and were very patriotic. They worked hard, attended church, and in his mechanical and electrical repair business, Edwin had a reputation for service to his customers and the community. I admired them. My Aunt Norma was the funniest lady that I have ever met. In my toughest times, I think *if I could only hear my Aunt Norma laugh one more time*. Uncle Edwin was a health nut before there was such a thing. He lived to be close to 100 years old. His deep voice could fill a cathedral with music. It still gives me chill bumps when I remember him singing, *Amazing Grace*.

At Dad's funeral, Edwin and my niece Teresa (the daughter of my brother Charles) sang together in the Victoria Catholic Cathedral and it was special at an otherwise sad time. Later, at the burial site that was just down the street from the Cuero High School football field, Edwin broke the somber mood when he pronounced "Well, at least Herbert can listen to those damned Cuero Gobblers on Friday nights." Dad was an avid fan of the Cuero football team. In 2018, the Cuero Gobblers won their fourth state championship in football.

Mom said that showing affection was just the difference between the German and the Irish. I loved both sides of my family, the paternal Cuero/Victoria branch, and the maternal Beeville branch. During my early years, when I thought of family, I was usually thinking about the Beeville family.

I have asked my granny to introduce herself and tell you about her house. She is the only person that loves that house as much as I do.

HELEN RUTH (MURRAY) MORROW, MATERNAL GRANDMOTHER (GRANNY)

"Only for a grandkid would I do this. I'm not a talker."

My name is Helen Ruth Morrow. To everyone other than family, I am Ruth. To my kids I am Mom. To my grandkids I am Granny. Almost everyone calls me Granny or Granny Ruth.

I have four wonderful children, two boys, and two girls. I currently have five grandchildren, three girls, and two boys. I am providing this little introduction for Dickie, my youngest grandson. Dickie is a persistent kid and I love him so I gave up and will talk for just a little while.

My husband PW and I are lucky that our children and grandchildren live close to our home on East Milam Street in Beeville Texas.

PW and I have a clear division of responsibility. If it is in the front yard or inside my home, I take care of it. I cook, I clean, I sew, I decorate and occasionally I paint for my pleasure. I also hug anyone who comes in my door other than PW when he stays too long at the tavern. PW takes care of the outside, except for the front yard, and major work that needs doing on the house. The only thing I take care of behind the house is my chickens because I don't trust PW enough to take care of them. I get some help with the chickens from grandkids whenever they think about it or when I ask. I think the chickens stay because they like me and my grandkids, or because they have just settled in the backyard. PW will not fix the chicken coop fence.

PW and I have an understanding. We will make sure everyone in our family knows that we are here for them. We have enough food, shelter, love, and support for anyone in need no matter what is going on in their life. PW will try to make sure we have the money to take care of anyone who needs help and I will make sure that our home is welcoming to all who come. I will feed them. I will make sure they have a safe and comfortable place to stay. I will make sure they know they are loved. I expect other members of the family to help me. Everyone always helps when I need it. I get most of the help I need without asking. I am not against talking if someone else is doing it and not too much. I get most of what I need with hugs, smiles, and sometimes a shared cookie or fried mashed potato sandwich.

My world is my home and my family. My home is where I take care of PW and myself. It is where I take care of children and grandchildren. It is where I practice my crafts. It is where I pray. Our home is not perfect, but it is better than any home I've had in my life.

It will be an answered prayer if I can live in this house for the rest of my days.

My entertainment, besides family and home, is not complicated or expensive. I like to quilt, and I like to express myself with paint. I also like for Billy, Gene or Herbert to take me fishing.

I am just about done talking. I will let my house and Dickie tell you anything else about Granny Morrow that might be of interest. I just have one more comment to make that I have already made to PW. I told PW, "Why don't you cut down that old windmill. It don't work and it's a near occasion to sin for the grandkids."

PW said, "It's my windmill. I'll cut it down if and when I get ready or when you cut down that old Live Oak tree in the front yard."

Dickie comes to me and says, "Granny, help me to not climb the windmill."

I say, "Shush, stop yourself."

GRAND OLD HOUSE

My Grandmother's home was the center of her universe. Helen Ruth (Murray) Morrow was a quiet lady who never stopped working unless she was fishing. Granny was the matriarch to the five families that lived close to her home. To me, her home was the Grand Old House. In truth, it was not as large as it seemed to me in those early days, and it needed repair that it would never receive because my grandparents were poor. We never heard them complain about anything, including money.

The old house was always spotlessly clean and had a fresh coat of paint. If that house could speak it would say:

I'm a Grand Old House. I'm a family home. I'm always full of children and they make me sing with their sounds. Out front, when you approach me, you will be immediately impressed with the huge Live Oak tree in my front yard. It has ropes hanging from the tallest limbs. My yard is full of children. Usually, my tree is full of children playing 'Tarzan and Jane' or some other loud game with laughter and sometimes a short period of crying. Tarzan or Jane falls, or someone swings too low on the rope that replaces the vine in the Tarzan movies. As you pass the tree, you come to my front porch. It always has several old rocking chairs. Usually, you will find Tarzan's or Jane's mom, or an aunt, ready to soothe hurt feelings, bandage skinned knees, or serve as a quiet referee to keep order.

As you pass through my big front door, you enter a small parlor that leads in three directions. In one direction a staircase leads to an upstairs apartment with two bedrooms, a bath and a large combined living room-dining room, and a kitchen.

Until they built their home next door, upstairs was home to Uncle Billy, Aunt Sue Ellen, and their daughters Ruth and Patricia.

Grand Old House

My masters, PW and Ruth, live downstairs. PW pretends to be in charge, but Ruth is my boss. Ruth lives up to her biblical namesake. She puts home and family first. That means I feel special and I get special care.

Now, for the tour. From the front parlor, if you take the door to the right, on the bottom floor, you will enter my living room. My sofas are draped with patchwork quilts, made by Granny Ruth. Granny is a person of few words, but you can tell by her actions that her home and her family are special.

To the left of the parlor is my master bedroom. Granny keeps the bedroom as a guestroom for any family members who might need to stay for a night or a week or longer.

Both the living room and master bedroom lead into the large dining room. The dining room serves as the living quarters for Granny and PW. Along one side of the dining room is a large long table that can seat the entire extended family. The table was built by Granny's sons Billy and Gene. The other side of the dining room houses Granny and Grandad's bed and a small corner for Granny's sewing machine. Directly behind the sewing machine is a door under the staircase. This holds a small closet for quilting and sewing supplies.

The only downstairs bathroom is off the dining room, directly behind the dinner table. PW knows that the downstairs needs an extra bathroom for guests. Guests need to go through the dining room, which serves as the private area for Granny and PW, to use the bathroom. Granny broached the idea of another bathroom.

PW responded, "Don't hold your breath. If I did that someone would move into that front bedroom to stay." A lot of folks in the family don't like the things PW says, but he usually speaks the truth.

Through the dining room is the kitchen, which spans the back of the house. The kitchen is Granny's favorite room. It is where she spends most of her time, cooking, canning, or preparing for the weekly ritual of Sunday Dinner.

On Sunday, we have the same basic menu: fried chicken, mashed potatoes and gravy, green beans, fresh-baked biscuits and pie. Granny makes all varieties of pies, but there is always at least one apple pie, the favorite of several children. Sometimes there is even a dip of homemade ice cream for the pie.

Granny Ruth is a quiet and reflective lady. However, she has another side that most people do not know about. Ruth is an artist. In her artwork, she is NOT quiet; she speaks in loud colors. Ruth's pallet is my kitchen floor, where she creates a new masterpiece each year. I am sure that she never heard of Wassily Kandinsky, a Russian artist who lived from 1866-1944. Kandinsky is considered one of the pioneers of Abstract Art. He is quoted as saying, "Colour is a means of directly influencing the soul."

In Beeville, Texas the Pioneer of Abstract Art is Granny Ruth

Morrow. Granny directly influenced her soul and the souls of her grandchildren during the annual painting of the Masterpiece. Granny was in a different world as she lay down paint streaks and spatters in very bright colors. When the masterpiece was just the way she wanted it, there was always a big smile. To her grandchildren, both the smile and the floor were beautiful.

During the painting ceremony, PW would always shake his head and say, "If you need help painting the kitchen floor, just ask." Granny spent a lot of time in the kitchen, so she spent time in the presence of her masterpiece. I am sure that when Granny moved up to heaven, she and Wassily Kandinsky discussed color and art.

No house and its mistress have ever loved each other the way I love Granny Ruth Morrow, and I believe the feeling is mutual. Dickie will have to tell you about the back yard. Granny has made it clear to me that the back yard is not part of the house. I have nothing to do with the back yard, and usually little to do with PW.

PW's Back Yard as seen by Dickie

The backyard has a windmill that lures children to climb, although it is strictly off-limits. That windmill caused lots of trouble for me. I was about five years old when I climbed to the top of the windmill. I loved to just sit on the top and survey the world. I could see the Bee County Courthouse. I could see church steeples. I could see cattle grazing. I loved the view and the quiet. I couldn't figure out why it was against the rules to climb the windmill. It was so much easier to climb than the Live Oak tree. I was always caught by Mom, who immediately picked a large switch from the salt cedar tree. Once, as I was climbing down to face the music, Grandad emerged from his paint room, and said, "Don't touch that boy! I told him he could climb the windmill." In the end, Mom was crying, I was crying, and Grandad got into his car to go to the tavern. Grandad asked me to come along. I loved going with Grandad to the tavern and holding his Stetson, but I knew today was not a good day. I did not get a switching, but I was bound to silence about the entire episode. I knew that if Dad found out, there might be more trouble.

I learned several lessons that day:

1. Breaking the rules and causing trouble between your Mom and your Grandad was bad business and was worse than a switching.
2. Grandad would always take my side, even when I was wrong. I vowed to not put him in that position again.
3. The windmill was thereafter always a temptation. I missed my quiet survey of the world.

Years later, as a lookout on a fleet submarine, I got my chance to survey the world again and I loved it. I thought, *If I could have got Granny to the top of the windmill, she would have loved it.* We always liked to share quiet places.

Dickie in the chicken coop

Just past the windmill was a barn, which housed a little bit of everything including Baby, the milk cow, and Ruth and Patricia's horse. PW kept his paint equipment in the barn. Granny kept the supplies for the chickens in the barn. Other members of the family contributed items to add to the barn's clutter. However cluttered, the barn seemed to be functional. Off to the side of the barn were the chicken coop and yard.

I loved hanging around with the chickens. This picture always leaves a lump in my throat. We were poor but didn't know it. I never wore shoes (except to church) until after I started school, and I would not wear shoes today if I could get away with it. Chickens were one of my connections with Granny. She always made me feel that I was responsible for raising her chickens and gathering the eggs. I'm not sure how I thought all of the chicken work got done while I was off doing other things. Granny had Rhode Island Reds and White Leghorns. I loved all the chickens, but to me the Rhode Island Reds were special. The Rhode Island Reds and the White Leghorns had little to do with each other. On Saturday evenings, PW would send whichever grandkid was available to catch two chickens so he could wring the necks in preparation for Sunday dinner. I sometimes felt guilty, but I always caught White Leghorns and never a Rhode Island Red.

World War II Disrupts the Beeville Family

Pearl Harbor was bombed two days before my third birthday. When Mom heard the news, she carried me around for hours whispering to me that all would be well. I know that she was thinking about her brother, my Uncle Gene, who was at Pearl Harbor. By the time I was five years old, World War II had completely disrupted my Beeville family and my life.

Grandad managed to keep the family business going during the war years after Uncle Billy and Uncle Gene enlisted. My Uncle Billy was the supervisor of the day to day business and was an expert painter. Together with Uncle Gene, they were the talent that kept the business going.

When Uncle Gene went into the Navy, and Uncle Billy joined the Army, I am not sure how Grandad kept the business going.

Somehow, Sunday dinners in the Grand Old House continued.

Grandad continued to dress in his starched khaki trousers, white shirts, and ties all with strategic paint spatters and Stetson hat. He continued to solicit new work. I know this because I often accompanied him and held his Stetson when he entered a house to give an estimate, or when we entered the tavern to catch up with friends and to talk about the war and their sons. We always had a few cool ones, root beer for me, and leads for new business. I loved the tavern and I loved the stories even though I did not fully understand the desperation these folks must have been feeling.

Uncle Billy in War Zone
1943

I don't think America did a good job of taking care of families while the breadwinners fought in World War II. Families were strong and seemed to take care of each other. Gene's wife, Alene, had her professional secretary job and had family in Beeville. Billy's wife, Sue Ellen, had a supportive family in Louisiana if she needed them. World War II did not miss their Louisiana family when it spread the trauma of war.

Dad was recruited by Humble Oil Company to take a truck and automobile repair job at the Humble Refinery in Ingleside, Texas. The job came with a draft deferment because of the critical role the refinery played in the war effort. The job also came with a company house and a pick-up truck so Dad could be close to his work. He was on call 24 hours a day, 7 days a week. I think everyone in the family was happy with how Dad would contribute to the war effort.

I remember that I resented having to leave Beeville to go to Ingleside. I felt I had lost everything except my parents. I lost my cousins, I lost my uncles, and I lost my grandparents. They were the family of my young life. While everyone did not think Dad's job contributed to the war effort, I know that Mom had already given up a lot with both of her brothers serving overseas and the move to Ingleside. This was the first time she had ever lived away from her parents. I believe that Dad did what he felt was his best contribution to the war effort. He was doing important work and he was a good worker. In Ingleside, Dad was still available to help the rest of the family, although it was an hour's drive away.

Our family was lucky. Uncle Gene came home from the Navy and began a successful flooring company. Uncle Gene eventually went to college using the GI bill. He became a role model for me, in a new way, as an adult returning to college. Uncle Billy fought in the European Campaign until the end of the war. He came home from the Army and assumed the lead role in the painting and interior decorating business. I was privileged to go with Ruth, Patricia, and Aunt Sue Ellen to Louisiana to welcome their Dad home from the war. He was, and is, a hero to me. I slowly adapted to the loss of my Beeville family when we moved to Ingleside.

2

INGLESIDE, TEXAS

1943-1946

HERBERT WITTE, FATHER (DAD)

"Just as I get the damned draft figured out, I upset my family by moving them to a town nobody has ever heard of."

Dickie asked me to introduce myself and tell you my World War II story before he tells you his story. The Beeville family has fallen apart. My brothers-in-law, Billy and Gene have joined the military. Billy is in Europe, as a GI, and Gene is a sailor in Hawaii. Except for the bombing, I think Gene got the better deal. PW Morrow, my father-in-law, and CG Witte, my dad, are too old to serve, so I'm the last one to try to figure out how I'll spend the war. I want to do what's right, but I don't want to leave what's left of the family, especially my son, Dickie, and my wife, Nannie Lee, with no one to take care of them.

Billy's wife, Sue Ellen, with her daughters, Ruth, and Patricia, could probably go to Louisiana, to her family, but that's not home. Plus, her Louisiana family has its wartime struggles. Alene, Gene's wife, has a family in Beeville, and she has a good job, so she is probably okay except for worrying about Gene. I don't know if PW is equipped to keep his business going without Billy and Gene and keep up the old house that serves as the center for family activities.

I believe that Dad, Mom, and my sisters will be okay. Dad has a good business doing electrical, refrigeration, and heating installation and repair. He's still strong and healthy. Mom is not in good health, but she is in good hands. My sister Marie takes good care of Mom.

My biggest worry, besides Dickie and Nannie Lee, is the Beeville family. I know that Granny Ruth and PW are stubborn, independent folks. While PW and I have words on occasion, I know that they like and trust me, and I probably have the skills to fix anything that might break.

In the back of my mind, I imagine people thinking, *He's just using these family responsibilities to avoid going into the military.*

I just get up every morning, work hard all day, and pray about what I should do.

Dad always said, "No decision is a decision."

He should know. He made a lot of 'no decision decisions' during the Depression. We all survived the Depression, so I decided to follow Dad's advice. I think this is the only time I ever followed my father's advice. Perhaps this is the first time I faced a decision as difficult as he did when his life collapsed around him. So, if the draft calls, I will go, and I hope they put me to work keeping those fancy war machines working. If they decide I need to carry a gun, I know how to do that. The Guadalupe River Bottom Squirrels will vouch for my marksmanship. Perhaps I could be a sniper. I am not great at taking orders, but whatever happens, will happen.

Humble Makes the Decision

One day, just as I was climbing out of my wrecker, this guy walked up to me and said, "Herbert, have you received your draft notice?"

I said no.

He said, "Well son, your government needs you to serve differently. Humble Oil needs to supply the fuel to keep America running, plus, all the ships, tanks, and trucks we need to fight the war. We need a journeyman mechanic and truck driver to keep our vehicles in the refinery in good working order. In exchange for your service, we'll match your current paycheck, plus give you a nice house on the refinery. We'll give you a pick-up truck to drive during your workday. The government will give you a draft deferment as long as you work for Humble. You'll need to move from Beeville to Ingleside. Fishing in Ingleside is good, and I know you love fishing. You'll be on call 24 hours per day, 7 days a week. But, so far, nobody has shot at our workers."

Working for Humble Oil was the answer to how I would serve. I knew America and her allies would win the war, and I knew I would contribute by working hard. Hell, work was about all I did well, other than hunting and fishing. My hunting and fishing buddies, Billy and Gene, were off in the military, doing a different kind of hunting. By working at Humble, I would be serving, but I would be doing work I loved. In an emergency, I would be available if someone needed help in Beeville or Cuero.

Nannie Lee seemed happy with the Humble decision at first, but she had a hard time being away from her mom. She also was overly sensitive to our son's constant complaining about leaving Beeville and the stupid kindergarten. I tried to keep quiet about issues I could not change. I agreed with Dickie about the kindergarten, but I wanted to tell him, "Just suck it up, son."

DICKIE'S INGLESIDE STORY

When I was five years old, my family moved from Beeville to Ingleside. In Beeville, I lived across the street from my grandparents and spent my days playing with my cousins. In Ingleside, there were no cousins or any other family except Mom and Dad.

Dad loved his job because it came with a house and a pick-up truck for work. He worked for the Humble Refinery, later to be ESSO and then EXXON. Dad was an auto mechanic and was responsible for keeping the Humble Oil trucks and cars in good working order. He was on call day and night, so we had to live in company housing on the refinery compound. Mom and Dad thought it was wonderful because it was free and was like a small community. I thought it was more like a prison because it was surrounded by an eight-foot fence and you had to have permission from the guard to get outside. Five-year-old kids never had permission to leave unless they were with their mom or dad. I missed my cousins and Granny and Grandad. They provided me with an endless supply of cookies and shoulders to cry on. I also had no chickens to feed and never got to go to the local tavern with Grandad.

Kindergarten was surrounded by a fence to keep the kids trapped inside. I was sent to kindergarten when I was five. I had a fear of school. I felt like Mom had dumped me so she could have coffee with her friends. I began to plan my escape. My plan included climbing the eight-foot cyclone fence with barbed wire across the top. The fence separated the kindergarten building from the housing area. When we were let out for recess, I hid in a corner of the playground, and when recess was over, instead of going back to class, I climbed the fence to freedom.

In getting over the fence I scratched myself on the barbed wire, (pronounced "bob war" in Texas.) Bleeding and afraid of the consequences of my escape, I climbed under the first available house until it was time for school to be out. Then I went home only to find that I was the focus of an all-out search. Mom was embarrassed and angry. Dad pretended to be angry, but I saw him chuckling.

I could have apologized and returned to kindergarten the next day.

I refused to apologize and was expelled from kindergarten. While kindergarten was an optional year of school in those days, Mom was traumatized by the whole event. Mom had me underfoot, again, which was where I thought I belonged. Mom was sure I would never succeed in school and for a time I was sure she was right. The only thing I regret about the kindergarten episode was that Mom did not live to see me graduate from college.

The next year, with the war ending and amid labor disputes, Humble Oil announced they were going to close the refinery. Dad was given the option of transferring to Baytown, Texas, a three and a half hour drive away, or accepting a severance package. Dad accepted the severance and we stayed in Ingleside. He used his severance pay to open an auto repair business behind Jack Clark's Service Station, and we bought our first home. The small house was across the street from Ingleside Elementary School.

During that summer, before first grade, I walked across the street to the school and talked to Mrs. Cook, the first-grade teacher. I told her about the great escape from kindergarten and my fear of school. She taught me how to clean blackboards and erasers and how to make copies on a mimeograph machine. She told me that I would be her helper and that I would have a lot of fun in first grade. I did. Ingleside eventually named an elementary school for Mrs. Cook. In 2019, Ingleside School System saved the façade of my school. Thank you for saving this doorway to my life of learning.

I do not remember much about this time in Ingleside. There were several noteworthy events. In first grade, I had a friend who lived next door and he was my first friend who was not a cousin. He had every toy known to man and had his toys meticulously organized. He always shared his toys. I learned a lot about organizing and sharing from my new friend. My only toys were my six-shooter cap gun and my fishing pole. I no longer had my Tarzan ropes hanging from the Live Oak tree at Granny's house and I no longer had my cousins to play with.

I survived the first of many storms in Ingleside. After the hurricane winds stopped blowing and the flooding stopped, Dad took a piece of tin that had blown off a roof and made me a canoe. I paddled around our flooded neighborhood for several days, barefooted, in what the neighborhood kids called our little ocean. Paddling that home-made canoe has always been a recurring happy vision of my childhood.

I always wished that I could recreate that scene and escape in a canoe and paddle around a quiet body of water. In middle age, I acted on my vision. I purchased an Old Town Canoe that I still have forty years later. I would strap my canoe to the top of my car and after a long workday, I would stop by a local lake and paddle around for an hour or so of quiet time. This was sort of like Grandad stopping at the tavern for a cool one after work. Like Grandad, a cool one occasionally made it into the canoe with me. I can no longer lift my canoe to the top of my car, but I can still drag it to the water's edge and climb in for a quiet break.

While my friend lived on the right side of my house, on the left side of our house was a small building that was sort of an unofficial school cafeteria. It was run by a lady named Jessie. Jessie was a friend to Mom and Mom loved working with Jessie to serve school lunches. I think Mom would have enjoyed a career outside the home, but that idea was not accepted by Dad.

One of Mom's special interests was to make the food we ate healthier, although she got little support from me or Dad. During the time we lived in Ingleside, she talked Dad into buying a Nannie goat. We were going to drink goat's milk which was cheaper than cow's milk and was healthier. I was not cooperative, and the goat butted Dad at every opportunity. I joined Dad in giving Mom an ultimatum. Sell the goat or the goat would be BARBEQUE. Jessie helped Mom find a buyer.

Jessie introduced us to Harry, who had an old Dodge pickup truck. Harry would pick me up and take me fishing. It was a great arrangement. Mom had time to visit with her new friend, Jessie, and I got to go fishing with a grown-up. For the first time, I think Mom and I both realized that friends could be family. Our Beeville and Cuero families were too far away for Sunday dinner, and some were overseas serving in the military.

Across the street from our little house lived the Ingleside School Superintendent, OT Blaschke. OT would one day teach me chemistry and taught me that a great educator is first a great teacher. No wonder

Ingleside had a great first-grade teacher like Mrs. Cook. OT's example did not escape any of his teachers. Ingleside has always had an exceptional school system with excellent teachers.

OT had a daughter, Laura, who was about the same age as my cousin, Ruth. Laura was just enough older than me that I assumed that she had no interest in playing with me and I certainly did not have time for girls. Many years later, Laura and I would serve together on the first board of directors of The Ingleside Ex's Alumni Association. The Ex's Association is now a thriving organization that provides fellowship among Ingleside Alumni (Ex's) and raises scholarship funds for deserving students. Ingleside School System is still an excellent school system and has one of its own as its Superintendent.

After first grade, Mom and Dad sold the house in Ingleside. Dad sold his auto repair business, and we moved around 90 miles to Cuero, Texas, where Dad grew up.

Nannie Lee (Morrow) Witte, Mother (Mom)

"What do you mean you hate kindergarten and you are never going to school again? Son, you are testing my patience." I wish Mom were here to talk to me. I am so lonesome.

Dickie asked me to introduce myself and give my thoughts on our time in Ingleside.

My name is Nannie Lee and I am Dickie's mom. I am the younger daughter of PW and Ruth Morrow. While 1943-1946 was a stressful time for our family and America, it was also a time to be thankful. I am thankful that I have a home for my family. I am thankful that my husband has a good job. I am thankful that we are safe and secure. I am thankful that I did not hear any bad news about my brothers, who served in the military overseas. I am also thankful that after the stress of the war, my parents are still safe and healthy.

While my husband worried a lot about what he should do during the war, I know he did what God intended him to do. It was a comfort to my brothers' families, and to my parents, to know that my husband, Herbert, was not overseas while my brothers were gone. The family appreciated Herbert and they knew that if it's broke, Herbert can fix it. I am thankful for the peace this gave to all of us.

My husband and my brothers are best friends. I sometimes think that Herbert married me so he could be closer to my brothers. Billy and Gene and Herbert love to hunt and fish together. I will be glad when they can be together again.

Most days I can manage a little space from Dad, PW, who is a handful. I miss Mom every minute of every day. I'm sure Mom is also missing me.

Dickie is the light of my life and, so far, my only child. In Beeville, with the help of my parents and his cousins, he was a joy. However, in Ingleside, he has been a challenge. You would think that he was the only one missing family. Herbert says, "Don't worry. He's a tough kid." He does seem to be settling in. I think we're all settling in. We're becoming our own family. Dickie and I have both made friends outside the family. We discovered that sometimes, friends are family. Herbert always seems to make work friends. I wish I could work outside the home.

The end of the war was a great relief, but it seems to have thrown Herbert into another work controversy. Should he take Humble's offer to move to Baytown? Should he take a severance package from Humble Oil and perhaps start his own business? I've decided that I have worried enough. Herbert is a good worker. Everyone wants Herbert as an employee. Whatever he decides about work will be fine with me and I know Dickie will be fine. Dickie seems to have made peace with school, thanks to Mrs. Cook and Ingleside Elementary School. Even though making friends is hard, Dickie and I both know we can do it. We'll be fine.

3

CUERO, TEXAS

1946-1950

CG Witte, Paternal Grandfather (Grandpa)

"I'm sorry, Officer, I had no idea that it was illegal to set off a fire alarm when there was no fire! Technically, I did not set off the alarm. The alarm was set off by the burglar. Perhaps I will modify the sound of the alarm, and we will call it a burglar alarm, a new invention. Then the police can come rushing to my house, instead of both the police and the fire department. It scared the hell out of the guy who broke into my garage."

Hello. My name is Charles Gregory Witte.

To my customers and my friends, I am CG. If you're my grandson, who I call Herr Dickie, I am simply Grandpa and that is my favorite name. I'm writing this little introduction for Herr Dickie. In Cuero, Texas, we spent a lot of time together. I am not a big talker, but Herr Dickie was a good listener, and he managed to get me to talk a

CG Witte

little each day. He asked me to introduce myself and to tell you a little bit about my Enough is Enough concept, which was learned through experience with success and failure. He also wanted me to share one of the adventures we experienced while he lived in Cuero.

I am a second-generation German American and a native Texan. My parents both left Germany for the freedom promised by America and to escape the politics of oppression and dominance that seemed to continue in Germany.

While my parents were both from Germany, they did not meet until they came to Central Texas. My parents were wed in Frelsburg, a small community in Colorado County, Texas and they had seven children. I was the baby. At home, we continued to speak German but learned English. As the youngest child, I lived with Mom after Dad passed, and before I began my working career.

The German American residents of the Frelsberg area, including my brothers and sisters, had a positive and significant influence on the history of Central Texas. The freedom to practice our faith was important to us (we were mostly Catholic and Lutheran), and we worked hard to help build a strong America.

As a kid, I was a good reader and I loved reading about the inventions that were changing America. I was also good at math and science. I believed that if I could imagine it, with math, science, and mechanics, I could build it. I did build quite a few things. Some called me an engineer, but I was an inventor. Some of my inventions became part of industrial machines like the cotton gin. What wealth I achieved out of these inventions I lost during the Great Depression, along with my pride and my desire for wealth. Thereafter, I simply became one of the early small businesses that combined the electrical trade with the growing demand for electrically controlled refrigeration, heating, and air conditioning. Within this trade, I was able to have enough financial freedom to support my family and continue my inventions as personal projects rather than to get rich. I have been able to apply my concept of Enough is Enough to money, work, faith, and all the other aspects of my life.

Herr Dickie loved my concept for money. For a while, I thought he was going to miss the point. But he settled in and it has served him well. I know he wants me to share my concept as it relates to money as many folks have trouble making peace with money. As simple, easy, and true as it is, most folks need to try it to believe it. You must develop the discipline to follow the plan. If you want to have enough, you need to do enough. That concept is as true for faith or happiness as it is for money. Some who have everything find faith and happiness elusive concepts. Like some of my inventions, my money plan seems to have caught on with many people. It is now a common recommendation, by folks who call themselves Financial Planners.

For money management, simply put ten percent of any money you receive from any source, tips, gifts, or money you earn into a Comfort Fund. I call it a Comfort Fund because the purpose is to give you and your family enough financial comfort so that focusing on the important things in life is a bit easier. This is not a wealth-building program. If wealth is a goal, you will probably need to take risks. I tried wealth as a goal and decided enough is enough.

I recommended using a big German Sour Pickle Jar to Herr Dickie when he started his Comfort Fund with Altar Boy tips. He could watch his comfort grow in the pickle jar. I am sure times have changed, use whatever works for you. God is good to us up here, but I have not seen a good sour pickle since I got here.

I believe many modern Financial Planners have modified my plan to recommend fifteen percent, rather than ten percent. I guess they are converting a financial comfort plan into a wealth-building program. I say enough is enough.

Although my friend PW Morrow and I only met once or twice on earth, we have become good friends in the afterlife. He was my grandson's maternal grandfather on earth. Since we have some of the same folks to watch over, we see each other often. We are both surprised that we made it to such a pleasant place. PW says he always knew about God's love, but he did not know that Baptists could take advantage of Purgatory as an alternative to Hell. We agree that Purgatory was bad enough. He said that my son, Herbert, told him that only Catholics could take advantage of Purgatory. Herbert said that Baptists with PW's drinking habits would probably go straight to Hell.

And yet, here we are! He was even more surprised that we could share a cold brew in the evening. He sometimes complains about the strict limits we have up here. A cold brew had not been his way on earth, but he says, "I know Enough is Enough in everything, not just money." PW is always giving me a hard time about Enough Is Enough, but it helped me find peace and comfort without always seeking more when I was on earth, and God seems to approve up here.

I had difficulty deciding which story to tell you from Herr Dickie's experiences with me during our brief time together in Cuero. I decided to tell you the burglar story. We were close then and we continue to be close today. He talks to me every day. I do not always answer him. I am not as busy as God, but He keeps me busy.

In those days, after I had stopped chasing the American Dream, my garage was my empire. I kept my 1935 Chevrolet Pickup (red with black fenders), in the garage along with many of my inventions, and inventions in progress. I have a lot of inventions in progress now that inventions are viewed as a hobby. I need to work on my closure skills or build a bigger garage.

One night a burglar broke into the garage. I am sure he was lured by tales that I buried my money because I didn't trust banks. He would never find my money. Instead, he ran headlong into my automatic washing machine.

I believe it was the first automatic washing machine. At the time, I had not solved the balance problem when the machine went into its spin cycle. So, I built a huge concrete form for the tub to keep it from walking during the spin cycle. The burglar stumbled on the concrete frame and fell into the tub.

When he recovered from the fall, he ran out of the garage, but he stumbled on the tripwire of my first attempt at a burglar alarm. I had used a surplus fire alarm to save a little money and the burglar alarm worked to perfection. The entire neighborhood thought there was a fire. The burglar continued his escape through my son Herbert's yard where Herr Dickie had left his new Western Flyer bicycle laying out in the yard instead of being put up in the garage. The burglar got tangled in the bicycle and broke his leg.

The police and the fire department responded. It was noisier than the Fourth of July. The family was angry, and Herr Dickie and I were both in trouble. Privately we thought it was funny. My reputation as a strange old inventor grew. The bicycle was repaired by his dad, who could fix anything. Dickie never left his bike out again. The burglar went to jail after recovering from the broken leg. In all the years I lived in Cuero, our neighborhood never had another break-in. I guess the burglar alarm idea must have been a good one. Although I lost interest in the automatic washing machine after I got it working, I understand it is standard these days.

Stay tuned for more stories from my grandson. I have told him to get busy. At 81, he will not live forever. I probably would have made it to 81 if they had not put me in that damned nursing home.

AMELIA (WENDEL) WITTE, PATERNAL GRANDMOTHER (GRANDMA)

| Amelia Wendel Witte, Herbert, Dickie and Nannie Lee

I was a challenge to Herr Dickie. I was older than anyone he had ever met. I was not in great health when he moved to Cuero. The one year we had together was special. When I moved up to the next level, I met his maternal grandmother, Ruth Morrow. Ruth and I spend time together, watching over our grandchildren. We know we were blessed.

Most grandmothers skip Purgatory after they leave earth. In our time, men made major decisions without input. With God's help, we made those decisions work. We did our penance on earth, so God let us take the high-speed elevator to the next level.

Some parts of my life were a challenge and a mystery. I'm going to leave the mystery of my life as a mystery. It is just history. When Dickie lived in Cuero, I was mostly confined to my bed. I was older than my years because of hard work and a productive life.

Almost every day when Dickie left school, he would come by to see me. When he got to our house, my daughter Marie would stop her work and brush my long silver hair while the three of us visited. Then we would pray the Rosary. That special time was a treasure to me. Marie worried about Dickie and she worried about me. Marie worried about everybody. I guess that is the reason she became such a caring nurse. Dickie seemed to have inherited the worry gene.

I was like the modern women of today. Life was complicated. I was thirty-three years old when my husband, Charles Gregory, and I were married. I was eleven years older than Charles, but we were in love. I was at an advanced age for childbirth, in those days, but we wanted a family.

My daughter, Norma was born the year after we were married. Two years later, my daughter, Marie, was born. My son Herbert, Dickie's Dad, came along a little later. Despite my late start, I had a wonderful life and a wonderful family. I told Charles that with all these kids I needed a better washing machine. He said, "I will build you one." I know he was working on that automatic washing machine when I passed. I am so grateful for the year I had with Dickie and my son Herbert after he moved back to Cuero.

Dickie seems determined to unravel my early life, and I will leave him to it. He has told me the old family story that my husband Charles rescued me from indentured servitude in the New Mexico

Norma, Herbert and Marie

Territory. I will not comment on that story. The important part of my history is that I married the great inventor Charles Gregory Witte and we had a wonderful family including Dickie. If Dickie needs a hobby in his retirement, he can investigate my history. I gave him some hints. When we meet again, we will compare notes.

Herr Dickie's Cuero Story

"I am finally home. I am going to live next door to Grandpa and Grandma. I am tired of moving. I will be a Cuero Gobbler just like Dad. Thank you, Lord."

We moved to Cuero after I completed the first grade in Ingleside. Dad became the Shop Foreman at the GMC dealership. I was impressed when they put an article about him and his new job in the Cuero newspaper. After the newspaper article, my Aunt Marie showed me pictures of Dad in his High School football uniform, his baseball uniform, and a picture of him throwing a shot put. She also showed me a letter from Texas Tech University offering Dad a scholarship. I noticed that this letter did not say anything about football, although Dad called it a football scholarship. Dad had been quite an athlete in Cuero and many still remembered him. After high school, Dad had

Herbert Witte in Cuero Letterman Sweater

a brief tenure as a baseball player, where he played catcher. I was given his catcher's mitt, but after a broken nose on my first day as a catcher, I was moved to second base.

Dad never really talked about his time as a high school football, baseball, and track team player, but he was deeply knowledgeable about sports. He told me that competition helped build character. While he loved sports in general, football was his game. Dad seemed proud of receiving a football scholarship offer from Texas Tech University. He said that college football would have been like a job, rather than a sport. He believed that football was a game to be enjoyed. Dad was my junior high school football coach when we moved back to Beeville. He believed competition and trying to win was important, but not more important than sportsmanship and learning to be a team player. To Dad, football was just a game.

The Cuero Gobblers were always strong competitors in Texas High School Football. According to the Cuero Heritage Museum, Cuero High School began its football program in 1911. They fielded many winning teams. The Cuero Gobbler football teams have always been a point of pride among ex-players and students. In 2018, the Cuero Gobblers won their fourth state championship at AT&T Stadium, home of the Dallas Cowboys. I hope Dad took time off from his duties upstairs to watch his beloved Cuero Gobblers win another football state championship. At Dad's funeral, his brother-in-law Edwin Boldt, said, "Herbert is right where he would want to be. He can listen to the Gobblers play and practice to his heart's content." In Cuero, the cemetery is right behind the football stadium.

I assumed that the move to Cuero was so it could be our permanent home. I thought I would be living next door to my Grandparents for the rest of my life. That would be OK with me. While I liked Ingleside, moving and making new friends was hard for me.

REFLECTIONS ON GRANDMA WITTE

Grandpa and I had many great adventures but my time with Grandma was much too short and a new situation for me. Grandma was bedridden when I came to Cuero and a year later, she was gone. I tried to spend time with her every day. I loved praying the Rosary with Grandma and Aunt Marie and I loved watching Marie lovingly care for her mother. As I spent time with Grandma, I wondered and worried about Granny in Beeville. She was always taking care of everyone else. Who would take care of Granny when it was her time to be close to the end?

I worried every day that Grandma might be gone when I got to her house. My short time with my beautiful Grandma was dominated by my fear of losing her before I got to know her. When I told Grandpa about my fear he said, "It's ok. I am still getting to know Amelia. We should be happy that she agreed to be part of our life. I know I will not get her automatic washing machine finished before she goes. She probably forgot about the washing machine." I knew she remembered the washing machine and loved Grandpa for working on it.

Grandma had soft hands and long silky hair when I knew her. Grandpa said, "She had working hands and shorter hair when we were younger. I loved that she could outwork most men." I am determined to learn more about this beautiful lady. I am sorry I did not spend more time with her.

I was sure that Cuero would be the home of my generation of the Witte family when Dad bought the entire block of empty lots behind Grandpa's house on the corner of East Valley Street. Mom and Dad picked the first lot behind Grandpa to be the location for our new home and Dad said we would keep the next lot to provide us some privacy. I was certain that he was saving that lot for me. He had the rest of the block platted into residential lots and sold them to help pay for our new house.

THE CUERO HOUSE

Our new house was not exactly new. Dad knew about a house that had been deserted out near the Guadalupe River during the Depression and then World War II. The house had been built with heart pine and had oak floors. Dad said, "This house is as solid as any house we could build, and we can make it into anything we want." Dad and Grandpa agreed.

Cuero House Nannie Lee Dickie and Western Flyer 1948

They laid out the measurements of the house on our lot and built a foundation. Then, we had the house moved to our lot and placed on the foundation. Despite some minor adjustments, Dad and Grandpa made the house fit on its new foundation. Who could doubt that two generations of German American Texans would not get it right?

Dad was also right in that it was a very solid house. We all helped with the cleanup. Dad installed new windows and doors. By the time the windows and doors were complete, Grandpa had installed an upgraded electrical system. One of Grandpa's plumber friends installed an updated plumbing system. Dad borrowed a floor sander from my Uncle Gene in Beeville and sanded the oak floors. In just a few months we were ready to move in. Dad worked on the house every day after his regular hours at the GMC Dealership. I cannot remember where we lived during the reconstruction and there is no one to ask. I am sure we did not live with Grandpa. That would've been too much to ask. Dad and Grandpa had an arms-length love. They loved each other but too close was too close.

While the house was not like the Grand Old House in Beeville, it was my favorite home for the Herbert Witte family during my childhood. I recently drove to Cuero to see if the house was still there, and to check my memory. The house is still there. It has been over sixty-five years since I last lived there, and the house was probably 35 years old when we moved it into town. Our little house is close to 100 years old.

It looked like a busy family now lived in the house. The yard and house were neat and tidy.

The house was a rectangle with the right half of the house serving as the living room, dining area and kitchen. The left side had two bedrooms and a bathroom. The house had a covered front porch with the front door leading into the living room. The living room was truly a living room.

We did most of our family activities in this room including eating our meals in the back half which served as the dining area. The living room also served as the guest bedroom. The kitchen was directly behind the living room. From the front of the house, on the left side, was Mom and Dad's bedroom. A large bathroom divided Mom and Dad's bedroom from the kids' bedroom. The bathroom could be accessed from either bedroom or the Living Room. This was a progressive design for the 1940s. I remember many discussions over the drawing prepared by Grandpa.

When we had overnight guests, the visiting parents slept on the living room couch and had access to the bathroom. The kids made pallets on the floor. No one seemed to mind that it was crowded because it was fun. It was like an indoor campout. In the kid's bedroom (I was the only kid at that time), I picked the linoleum pattern from Sears and Roebuck. I chose a pattern that had games like checkers and monopoly. Friends and cousins could play games on the floor while the grown-ups played 42 with dominoes.

After World War II, my Beeville uncles came to visit in Cuero with their families because the Guadalupe River made for great fishing and the river bottom, with huge pecan trees, made for great squirrel hunting. My cousins Ruth and Patricia and I often accompanied the adult sportsmen.

Witte Catfish - Early 1940s. Patricia, Catfish, Dickie, Herbert, Billy

Witte Catfish Early - 1960s. Dick, Madonna, Jerrie, Catfish, Charles

We had our fishing equipment and guns. We were young for guns, but we respected our weapons and had been taught gun safety since about age six. The guns were usually 22 caliber rifles, although I believe that one of us had a 22-caliber pellet gun.

During one family visit, my Uncle Billy complained that he didn't care how good the hunting and fishing was; if Dad didn't fix the noisy refrigerator so he could sleep, he was never coming back. He was joking, but the next week, a brand new PHILCO refrigerator arrived. Keeping our home ready for visiting family and friends was important to everybody in my family. To our parents and my family, our home is a place that, when you get there, they are going to welcome you in and feed you, even if you have to sleep on a folding couch or a pallet on the floor. Folks do not seem to be willing to rough it these days, and I'm a little spoiled myself.

Mom was pleased to have her first new kitchen appliance. When the Philco arrived, everyone came to see the new refrigerator. Grandpa had an identical Philco delivered to his house the next week. He said he got a good price, which was the only reason he replaced the icebox at his house. My Aunt Marie lived with her parents and managed their household. Marie was glad to see both the icebox and the Ice Delivery Man become part of history.

Charles and the New Philco Refrigerator

Behind the house, we had a large backyard. This yard would eventually be the home of my first pet, a collie named Laddie.

LADDIE

When it seemed clear to me that Cuero was going to be home, I wanted a pet. Specifically, I wanted a collie puppy that looked like Lassie.

I campaigned for a dog at least as hard as I would later campaign for a Western Flyer bicycle. Mom said I always wanted something (other than a piano). Dad must have met Grandpa Witte's Enough is Enough criteria because Laddie came to me as my first pet when I was in the third grade.

I loved Lassie. I admired all that Lassie did for her family. When my baby collie arrived, he did look like a baby Lassie. Dad insisted that if we were going to have a Damn Dog it had to be a male dog. Females always got into trouble. I was not sure what trouble he was talking about, but I was happy to have a dog that looked like Lassie. I was sure my dog could do all the things Lassie could do. Mom said that only a

Dickie, Laddie and 1938
Ford -1948

female dog should be named Lassie, so I would need to pick another name. Mom suggested Laddie. I thought, *whatever you say, Mom, just give me my dog*. I said, "What a great idea Mom. Laddie, it is." Within the first weeks, Laddie was referred to as Damn Dog more often than Laddie. Laddie was a thief. He would show up carrying laundry from the neighbor's washroom, stray shoes, food, and anything else he could find.

Based on Laddie's reputation as the neighborhood thief, a decision was made. Laddie would lose his freedom to roam. Dad spent the next two weekends building a fence around the backyard where Laddie would live. In those days, dogs were never allowed in the house. Laddie grew rapidly and soon he had worn a path running circles around the backyard. I found out that having a dog was not all fun. My jobs, other than playing with Laddie, were to pick up his poop and feed him his daily ration of canned dog food. Mom told me I needed to train Laddie.

Nannie Lee Training Laddie – 1948

I thought to myself, *my schedule is already tight. Maybe Mom could train Laddie.*

Mom's relationship with Laddie soon soured and never recovered. Mom hung her favorite red corduroy blazer on the clothesline and Laddie could not resist. He not only made the red corduroy blazer into a toy, but he ate a good bit of it and there were more than a few piles of poop laced with red corduroy decorating the backyard. Now Laddie was referred to by two members of our little family as Damn Dog.

Laddie got one more chance. Dad built another fence, splitting the backyard into two parts. Mom got the front half of the yard for clotheslines and as a clean area for the family. Laddie was confined to the back half of the backyard. He was unhappy. I was unhappy. I had to go all the way to the back of the backyard to play ball with my dog. I began to fall behind in my poop scooping duties. Laddie became a chore. It was a chore I was not good at. I still feel guilty for neglecting my wonderful dog Laddie.

When the Witte family moved back to Beeville, I believe Laddie stayed behind in Cuero. Hopefully, Laddie went off to live on a farm where he was free to chase rabbits, squirrels, and cats or just lay in the shade. The luster of dog ownership had worn a little thin on me. Mom and Dad insisted that they would be happy without any pets. I hope Laddie had a happy second life.

————

The Victoria Family

With a new house and a new job, Mom and Dad seemed happy. Mom decided to convert to Catholicism. I think St. Michael's Catholic Church in Cuero won her over. There is something special about St Michael's and the folks who go to church there.

Once each week we traveled to Victoria for Mom to take instructions in the Catholic faith. While we were there, we would have dinner and visit with the Victoria side of Dad's family. This included his sister Norma, her husband Edwin Boldt, and their three sons, Francis, Bernard, and Bobby. The Boldt family was amazing to me. In many ways, they were like Dad. They could fix or even build almost anything mechanical or electrical. What I remember most about that time was the motorbikes that the Boldt boys built and rode all over Victoria. Mom refused to let me ride on the motorbikes, but I became proficient in regular bicycle riding as I tried to keep up with my older cousins. I wanted to be a man with a bicycle. I wanted to be a man on the loose. I wanted a bicycle like the Western Flyer at the Western Auto Store in Cuero.

————

Western Flyer

I began my campaign for a bicycle after my experience with my Victoria cousins. I assumed Dad could build me a bike from scrap parts so that it would not cost much. I coveted the Red Western Flyer that proudly sat in front of the Western Auto Store. I would go by the Western Auto Store at least once a week and inspect the Western Flyer. Then, I would drop hints to Dad about the things I wanted on my bike if I ever got one. I wanted it to be red, like Grandpa's pickup. I wanted it to be a full-size bike that would last for my whole life. I also needed it to have a light in case I had to go out at night to run errands for the family. My accessory list went on and on, just like the list for the new cars and trucks. I figured that if Dad could build me a full-size bike, I could add accessories a little at a time.

Dickie's Red Western Flyer Bicycle (Big Red)

You can imagine my surprise when the Red Western Flyer, with all its accessories, was sitting on our front porch on Christmas Day. I figured that there must be a Santa Claus because I knew Dad would never part with that much money. Now, of course, I know there is a Santa Claus.

I named my bike Big Red, the name I had secretly given to Grandpa's red pick-up truck. His truck was a 1935 Chevrolet with the commercial accessory cover in the bed. The truck was red with black fenders. The commercial cover was an original accessory in 1935.

The cover had a solid cab height top with canvas roll-up sides. Grandpa could have his work items for his electrical, heating, and

Similar to Grandpa's Red 1935 Chevrolet Pickup Truck (Big Red)

commercial refrigeration business in the sides of the bed and just roll up the canvas to have access. Grandpa told me, "A man needs good transportation, a good bike, and eventually a good truck." I often wondered if Grandpa had a role in me getting the Western Flyer. When I asked my Aunt Marie, she said Grandpa squeezed a dime so hard that it would bleed, so she doubted that he contributed to the bike. I decided that he probably campaigned Santa and Dad. I kept Big Red until at least high school, where I assume it became parts for my brother, Charles, who also could fix or build anything.

The Break-In (Herr Dickie's Version of the Story)

Next to our house in Cuero, Dad left a vacant lot to give us privacy. Our block developed quickly after Dad put the extra lots on the market, and we soon had next-door neighbors. I was responsible for mowing our yard, but Dad said we could let the vacant lot grow to give us more privacy. When Mom and the folks who built next door to the vacant lot became friends, I was required to mow a path through the lot for Mom and the lady next door to visit. One of my jobs was to help keep the path clear so that, when the neighbors visited at night to play 42, no one would get hurt. Mom said she didn't want anybody breaking a leg trying to visit. We had no streetlights, or other outside lights, except porch lights.

One night, about a year after we finished the house, a burglar broke into Grandpa's garage. This was a dangerous act. The garage was full. It had Grandpa's truck and all the electrical, refrigeration, and heating equipment for Grandpa's business. The garage also had many of Grandpa's inventions, including the first automatic washing machine. His washing machine had a tub built into a huge concrete box so that the washing machine would not shake or move when it was in the spin cycle.

The thief was busy looking around in the dark when he tripped on the washing machine's concrete box and fell into the tub. When he got out, he attempted to escape, and one of Grandpa's other inventions, a burglar alarm with a tripwire, was his downfall. The burglar tripped the wire and when the alarm when off he tried to escape through our yard. When he got to the vacant lot, I had left my bicycle in the path. The burglar broke his leg and ruined the front wheel of my new Western Flyer. The burglar went to jail, but I also got punished. I was grounded for leaving my bike out. Mom said she knew someone was going to break a leg in that path through the weeds. I had to start mowing the empty lot.

Grandpa's reputation as an eccentric inventor escalated after the

Cuero Fire Department and the Cuero Police Department arrived. Grandpa explained and apologized for using an old fire alarm.

The Fire Department was still unhappy. They said it was against the law for Grandpa to use a fire alarm for his burglar alarm. Grandpa didn't seem to care. His burglar invention worked. Even though I was in trouble, I loved the whole episode. My Grandpa was one-of-a-kind, and I loved all his inventions.

REFLECTIONS ON GRANDPA WITTE

Living in Cuero, Texas was a happy time for me. I loved living close to Grandpa and Grandma Witte and my Aunt Marie. Grandpa promised that I could have his big red truck after he was gone. By the time Grandpa stepped off the escalator, to his next adventure (heaven, I assume), I was off chasing Commie Thugs to Keep America Safe. I thought about how much I would miss my conversations with the man everyone said didn't talk. I realized I could keep on talking to Grandpa. He didn't need to answer.

On occasion, in the quiet, as I share some concern, I hear that little sound he made to let me know he was listening when I thought he was asleep. I know his new duties include keeping a check on a lot of folks, including me. The world has changed, but the pointers he gave me seem to be universally true. For example, Grandpa did not like money. He thought it was a necessary evil. If you had too much, it took over your life. If you had too little it could make you and your family suffer unfairly. He said he had experienced both extremes. He said the key was his Enough is Enough plan. With enough, you can focus on the important things, like meaningful work, family, faith, helping others and always learning. One of his enough pointers that I have tried to follow was to save ten cents from every dollar I earned from work or received in tips or presents. I started out using the big Sour Pickle Jar that he gave me. If I did this, he said I would never be broke.

Like Grandpa, I went through a period in my early adult years when I thought I was too poor to pay myself. I told Grandpa.

He said, "You missed the point."

That ended the conversation. I started feeding the pickle jar and made it back from not enough to enough. With that exception, I have continued to feed the institutions that took the place of the Pickle Jar. I have met enough criteria without ever having to focus on money. Enough is Enough.

Grandpa never trusted banking institutions after the Great Depression.

One vision I have that makes me smile is seeing Grandpa digging a hole in the dirt floor of his garage and putting something wrapped in an old towel in a box under the area where he parked his pickup truck. It does not matter where you put enough money if it makes you feel secure. I hope no one ever dug up his garage floor. I know he smiles when he thinks about his box and who might eventually find it.

My wife Jerrie recently came home from her Yoga class and told me about the class topic of Contentment. (Santosha in Sanskrit). She showed me the reading that her instructor, Joy Vera, shared at the end of class. Jerrie commented, "Your Grandpa Witte could have written this."

I talked to Joy about Grandpa Witte. We agreed that Grandpa was probably a Yogi without knowing it. Joy's reading explained Grandpa Witte's concept very well.

Joy's Reading

- I wish you enough sun to keep your attitude bright no matter how gray the day may appear.
- I wish you enough rain to appreciate the sun even more.
- I wish you enough happiness to keep your spirit alive and everlasting.
- I wish you enough pain so that even the smallest of joys in life may appear bigger.
- I wish you enough gain to satisfy your wanting.
- I wish you enough loss to appreciate all that you possess.

- I wish you enough.

SAINT MICHAEL'S CATHOLIC SCHOOL

Saint Michael's Catholic Church – Cuero, Texas

Cuero was a community that valued education, and Cuero always had a high percentage of German Americans who valued work, church, and school. A group of these residents built The English-German School about 1880. This old school building is being preserved by the Heritage Museum. Another school with a long history in Cuero is St. Michael's Catholic Elementary School. St. Michael's operated for much of the twentieth century and is still going strong in 2020. I would come to know St. Michael's very well.

My fear of school raised its head again when we moved to Cuero. In Cuero, I would attend St. Michael's Catholic Elementary School. This was the same school that Dad and his two sisters attended. I was to be taught by nuns. I had never seen a nun. Sister Agnes was in charge and seemed to me to be ancient. Sister Agnes had a good memory and she remembered Dad's years with her. She said that while Dad's sisters were angels, he was a challenge. She told me that, in her experience, fathers and sons often shared some bad habits. She said she would be watching me, even when I could not see her.

I realize, now, that Sister Agnes was an amazingly effective School Administrator. She was my first encounter with the Good Cop - Bad Cop management style. Sister Agnes was the Bad Cop and my second-grade teacher, Sister Anne Marie, was the Good Cop. Sister Anne Marie was one of the kindest creatures on earth. When I confessed to Sister Anne Marie my fear of Sister Agnes and school in general, she suggested that I turn all my fears over to God.

St. Michael's Catholic Church was just across the street from St. Michael's Catholic Elementary School, and in those days, the church was open anytime you wanted to stop by for a visit with Jesus. The church was a beautiful sanctuary and would bring even a non-believer close to God. I prayed at Mass before school every day. I spent a few minutes of my lunch hour in private prayer. After school, I stopped by for a quick visit with God before I walked home to visit with Aunt Marie and Grandma. I prayed that Grandma would be healthy again. At first, I believe my prayers just replaced my quiet time that was missing without my daily visits with Granny in Beeville. I also wanted to impress Sister Agnes and Sister Anne Marie. At some point, God, Sister Anne Marie, or St. Michael's church won me over. I privately began to believe that someday I would become a Catholic priest or perhaps a Baptist Minister at my cousin's church in Beeville. Although I never said this to my Aunt Marie (Catholic), or my Aunt Sue Ellen (Baptist), I was still having trouble seeing the difference between Catholics and Baptists, since we all worshiped Jesus Christ.

I decided to ask the ultimate source. Dad said, "As Catholics, we were the first Christians and therefore we had a head start in building beautiful churches like St Michael's.

We also collected lots of art over in Rome. Jesus was probably impressed and made us his favorites. Because we were his favorites, he gave us Purgatory. If we are not ready for heaven when we die, we stop off in Purgatory, which is not as hot as Hell. After a brief stay in Purgatory, sort of like one of our camping trips, we go to Heaven. Baptists, when they die, if they were not quite ready for heaven, they go straight to HELL." Dad continued, "Catholic Priests are more efficient than Baptist Ministers. They speak in Latin and we don't speak Latin anyway, so they go faster, and we complete Sunday Services in one hour or less instead of the minimum of two hours that it takes the Baptists."

As far as Dad could tell, the only advantage to being Baptist was that they eat fried fish any time, while Catholics tended to only eat fried fish on Fridays unless they were camping.

The whole Catholic and Baptist issue was resolved. I decided that Catholicism was right for me. I received my First Communion that year, in Second Grade, and that was my ticket to Altar Boy. I loved being an Altar Boy. I particularly enjoyed serving at special events such as High Mass, Benediction, Stations of the Cross, weddings, and funerals. It was a highlight of my childhood.

In modern times, girls have joined the server ranks and instead of Altar Boys and Altar Girls, we are all Altar Servers. I am not sure why more young folks don't serve.

BUDDING ENTREPRENEUR

During my years in Cuero, the need to supplement my allowance was clear. Thank goodness God was a big help. I was a popular Altar Boy for both funeral and wedding ceremonies. The tips for both could be quite substantial. I was comfortable with the families involved in weddings and funerals. I would have been glad to serve them without the tips, but the tips were nice.

It was by pure accident that I discovered how much I enjoyed sharing the company of ladies who were the age of my grandmothers. Just across the street from Grandpa and Grandma lived a widow lady named Mrs. Cowgill who owned several milk cows and provided most of the neighbors with milk, cream, buttermilk, clabber, and butter. I enjoyed visiting with Mrs. Cowgill. Our visits evolved into me performing some of the small chores required to produce her products. Eventually, I delivered her products to several houses in our neighborhood.

Mrs. Cowgill rewarded me for my efforts by paying me in milk and buttermilk. We loved her milk as it had more cream than store-bought milk, and Dad loved her buttermilk. Mom paid me for the milk and buttermilk, so I converted my efforts into cash. Almost everyone in the neighborhood gave me a small tip for delivering. On top of good cash flow, I loved being with Mrs. Cowgill and there were always hot cookies and cold milk at her house.

Another lady from the neighborhood was Mrs. Smith. She had a large house on a corner lot. Her entire lot was covered with pecan trees. I felt the same way about Mrs. Smith as I did Mrs. Cowgill. Since my Grandma Witte was an invalid, and Granny Morrow was in Beeville, I needed all the grandmother figures I could find. My work with Mrs. Smith was seasonal, although we visited year-round. During pecan season, I picked up pecans and we worked to bag them for sale. I got paid one bag of pecans for every ten bags we packaged. I also delivered pecans in the neighborhood. By the time I was in the fourth grade, I began to mow her yard. By word of mouth, I eventually had several yards in our neighborhood that I mowed. None of these jobs paid big money, but I almost always had money for the Saturday Matinee and a cone at Dairy Queen.

CUERO, THE TURKEY CAPITAL OF THE WORLD

When I was growing up in Cuero in the 1940s, it was an accepted fact that Cuero was the Turkey Capital of the World. By the early 20th Century, Cuero was shipping more turkeys than any other location in the nation.

Cuero had all the elements necessary to support the nation's increasing demand for turkeys. Cuero had ample processing centers, cold storage facilities, railroad connections to all the major commercial centers, and ample open land and natural food to support a huge population of hearty, healthy field turkeys. These turkeys could be herded to the processing centers much like cattle.

TURKEY TROT

Unofficially, the Turkey Trot began in 1910, when over one thousand turkeys were herded thirteen miles to the processing center by a small group of men on horseback. Turkeys are not as gentle as your average cow, so herding them was not an easy task. *Turkeyboys* needed more patience than the average Cowboy. However, the process of how to get these hearty turkeys to market was begun. In my childhood, the Turkey Trot was an exciting event for kids, young and old. Eventually, the Turkey Trot became a celebration that had a statewide following, and then a nationwide following.

The Turkey Trot Parade had as many as 40,000 turkeys parading down Main Street. One year the Texas Governor led the Parade. In 1972, news correspondent Charles Kuralt did a piece on the Turkey Trot that was on the National Evening News. Mr. Kuralt suggested that a turkey's intellect was so deficient that the Turkey Trot had to be held on a day when it was not raining. He believed the turkeys were not smart enough to stop drinking rainwater and would drown on the streets of Cuero, ruining the Turkey Trot. Mr. Karalt had not met the turkeys who roam my Texas neighborhood. Every day, these turkeys train hundreds of residents to let them direct traffic on busy streets.

The fear of turkeys dying on the streets was one of the factors that led to the end of driving turkeys to market. The move toward raising the newer 'broad-breasted' turkey in captivity did not include a proper aerobic program to prepare them to compete with the field turkeys. There was a genuine fear that these good looking, broad-breasted birds would drop dead on the streets if they were herded several miles.

The processing of turkeys is still a major industry in Cuero. The Turkey Trot has been replaced by The Turkey Feast, which Wikipedia refers to as a Turkey-Centric event. The event includes a Turkey Race, with turkeys from as far away as Wisconsin. My neighborhood turkeys suggest that it would be difficult to get in shape if they lived in Wisconsin, so they are going to stick to Texas, where they can run, just for the fun of disrupting traffic. I'm glad I have my own daily Turkey

Trot, although some neighbors might not agree. Perhaps it's because they do not have the same memories of watching thousands of turkeys strut their stuff on the streets of Cuero.

Cuero, A Center for Music and Dance

I never noticed music or dance in Beeville or Ingleside. I was occupied with World War II, escaping from kindergarten, surviving my first hurricane, and having my first friend who was not a cousin. In Cuero, music seemed to be important to everyone, and dance was fun.

My first encounter with music was not a positive experience. Mom decided that I needed an interest besides bicycles, ball games, hunting, fishing, squirreling away Dairy Queen money, and hanging out with Grandpa in his garage. She talked Dad into buying a piano and paying for piano lessons. I had no interest. It was just a chore that I had to do to stay out of trouble. Dad said, "If I have to pay, you have to practice." Most days, my piano teacher simply shook her head and patted my shoulder. Other than the names of the notes and where I could find middle C, the best I could do was memorize a couple of tunes. I pretended I was reading the music at my first and only music recital.

Everyone taking lessons had to participate in the recital. After the recital, I threw myself on Dad's mercy. I begged and he conceded. He said, "We've both given it our best shot." In addition to the money, Dad had to endure the practice in our small house after he completed his workday. He said, "Mom will get over it and we'll sell the piano." I think Mom and the piano teacher were relieved. Still, the piano sat there as a reminder of money not well spent. The piano and piano lessons added to my failure list. Mom reminded me of my failed dog training efforts every time Laddie got in trouble. Poor Laddie. I never taught him a single Lassie trick. I was beginning to feel his pain.

My friend Charles stopped by our house one day and saw the piano. He said, "Great looking piano. Can I play it?" Within minutes he had the house rocking with Boogie-Woogie. An endless stream of music came out of his fingertips. I could see Mom was almost crying. She had envisioned that I would be the piano player that Charles was naturally. The good news was that I discovered that I loved music, even if I was not able to play a musical instrument. I loved the fact that music made me feel good and made me want to dance to the beat. Charles and his family were all involved in music and he helped us sell the piano.

With the piano gone and my newly discovered love for music and dance, a new world opened. Charles and I had been playground pals. As we became closer friends, and I visited his home, I discovered that his whole family played and celebrated music and dance. In turn, I learned that Mom and Dad loved to dance but had just let it slip away during the war.

On weekends, Dad started taking us to dance halls where the entire family was welcome. The dances were held in barn-like structures. The adults could have a beer outside the dance hall and other beverages and snacks were also available. There was a dominance of Polka, Waltz, Country, and a little Boogie-Woogie. I can never remember anyone getting into trouble at the dance halls.

The memory of the Lindenau Dance Hall in Cuero is vivid in my mind. I could probably give you a tour. You need to go find a dance hall and give it a try. While I still cannot play a tune on any instrument, I often dream that one morning I will wake up and be able to sing and yodel like Narvel Felts.

THE CHICKEN NOODLE SOUP EPISODE

My first MORTAL SIN was better known as 'The Chicken Noodle Soup Episode.'

I normally think of myself as an optimist. But on reflection, I have a couple of weak links. One of those is the whole Heaven vs. Hell issue. In some belief systems, one false step and a lifetime of good deeds could end with a can of Chicken Noodle Soup, consumed by accident, on a Friday.

When I was a child, I was very concrete in my belief systems. My children would probably say that I am still concrete in my belief systems. I had two spiritual advisors who did not always agree on certain technical issues that were important to reaching Heaven and avoiding Hell. One of these spiritual advisors was my Aunt Sue Ellen, of the First Baptist Church, and the other was my Aunt Marie, who was Catholic.

As a First Baptist, dancing was a clear danger. In the Catholic faith, eating meat on Friday was a fatal flaw. A mortal sin, once and done, burn forever in Hell.

I took these issues very seriously. I attended confession every Friday and received communion every morning. Then the **SIN** slipped in.

One Friday morning Mom put chicken noodle soup in my lunch thermos and a fried egg sandwich in my lunch bag. I recognized the taste of the soup because it was one of my favorites. I consumed all the soup before I realized it was Friday. **THE DEED WAS DONE!!!!** Unless I made it to Confession before I died, I was going straight to Hell, and Confession was not until next Friday.

I was so careful riding my bike. No hands-high with feet on the handlebars as I sped down Old Victoria Highway. What was I going to do? I could not confront Mom and tell her she was sending her only son to Hell because she had sent him to school with a fatal soup. That wouldn't help. What other options did I have?

1. I could schedule an early Confession. But then, my whole class would know I had committed a Deadly Sin.
2. I could talk to Grandpa Witte. But his answer was always the same. "Don't worry about it. God would know it was a simple mistake."
3. I could talk to my Aunt Sue Ellen who would have a similar thought, only she would call it a Silly Catholic Rule.
4. I could talk to my Aunt Marie, but I knew what she would say. She thought like me. She would probably say, "Better

luck next time, and hope for no fatal accidents before Friday."

On Tuesday, I was saved by a Saint, who was also my teacher.

Sister Anne Marie noticed that I was not my jolly self and that I had skipped Communion the last two days.

She said, "What's going on?" I spilled the whole Chicken Noodle Soup Episode. She said as if she had heard this story every day, "There is no real chicken in Chicken Noodle Soup. They just take a small piece of chicken and they dip it in a large vat of soup. God would never count that as meat. I swear on Mom's grave, you have not committed a mortal sin because of your lunch last Friday. So, unless you have done something else that I don't know about, I expect you to be in line for Communion tomorrow morning."

Since we all know that Saints don't lie, Hell was narrowly avoided. Just to be sure, when I was still alive on Friday, I confessed the soup.

I finally came around to thinking like Sister Ann Marie and Grandpa, on matters of faith. Grandpa Witte is an important role model in almost every aspect of my life.

THE DESK CARVING EPISODE

The Desk Carving Episode was my first major Black Mark with Sister Agnes. In fourth grade, I became fascinated with the pocketknife carvings on the ancient old desks that we used in our classrooms. I decided to add DW with a date to my desk. Just as I got started with my project, I became aware that Sister Agnes was watching me. She took me to her office and gave me what today would be called corporal punishment.

I did another of my school escapes. I ran straight to the GMC dealership, where I told the story of the punishment, but not the crime, to everyone who would listen. Most of the workers agreed that the punishment was unfair. Dad told me to take off the rest of the day while he resolved the issue. Sister Agnes had a serious discussion with

Dad, and I got into very bad trouble for carving the desk. I surrendered my pocketknife to Dad for the rest of the school year. For a kid in South Texas to be without his pocketknife was almost like being naked. I also knew Sister Agnes was watching my every move.

THE TRASH TALKING EPISODE

The Trash Talking Episode occurred during a school-sponsored softball game with my sometimes friend David. He was pitching for the Blue Team and I was the batter for the White Team. David was a trash talker even before there was such a thing as trash talk. Since Grandpa Witte called me Herr Dickie and Cuero was a small town, I was Dickie at school. David started his trash talk from the pitcher's mound.

"What kind of a sissy name is Dickie anyway? I never saw Dickie in the Bible. Your baptism is probably bogus, and you're going straight to Hell, and I'm going to strike you out right now."

The Going Straight to Hell was the final straw. I threw down my bat and marched to the pitcher's box and threw a right uppercut that caught David on the chin. Within seconds there was a free for all between the Blue Team and the White Team.

Sister Agnes had her chance to get even with me over the desk carving episode, and she already had a long list on David. The rest of the teams received no punishment, but David and I had to spend recess helping Sister Agnes in her office. By the time Sister Agnes allowed us to return to recess, David and I were good friends and we had even gotten a couple of chuckles out of Sister Agnes. While David and I did not become best friends with the top nun, we never had any more trouble with Sister Agnes.

DAIRY QUEEN COMES TO CUERO

I ate most of my meals at home. Going to a restaurant was a foreign concept to me. I knew that when I went to the tavern with Grandad, PW Morrow, they sometimes served pretzels, and on rare occasions, peanuts with your beer or root beer. Ice cream only came from a machine that was hand-cranked on the front porch and only served on special occasions. Milkshakes and malts were extremely rare treats served at the Soda Fountain after the Saturday Matinee. A milkshake cost more than the movie and popcorn.

Downtown Cuero and the movie theater were not on my daily bike ride. My friends and I spent our time at each other's houses or a field where we could play ball.

The Dairy Queen was different. It was right on the Victoria Highway where my friends and I rode our bikes. Even the parents seemed to like Dairy Queen because making homemade ice cream was very labor-intensive. Dairy Queen lured you in with a new kind of ice cream (soft serve) in a five-cent cone. The convenience and the price lured in some financially conservative folks like Grandpa, who was known, on occasion, to spring for a foot-long hot dog and an ice cream cone.

Dairy Queen even supplied us with bike racks. With my Altar Boy money, I was able to drop-in and have a 5-cent cone after the latest ball game.

Cuero was excited to welcome the Dairy Queen. I believe the town even had a parade. Right now, I can't think of anything better than a foot-long chili dog and a Dairy Queen milkshake. I am glad to see that Dairy Queen seems to be doing well, over 70 years after Grandpa and I had our first foot-long and cone. Here in Georgetown, Texas, in 2020, the Dairy Queen even gives our Veterans a discount. You can't beat good food and patriotism.

MY BROTHER CHARLES COMES ALONG

In the fall of 1948, about the time school started, Mom broached the subject of a new addition to our family.

She asked, "You know how you told me that you were praying for a little brother or sister?"

"Yes, I prayed for a baby brother, but not a baby sister. I wanted a playmate to share my room, to go fishing, to play checkers, to help me take care of Laddie, and to go on bike rides. I had no interest in a baby sister. You would need to build another room because I would not want to share my room with a girl. Besides, it's too late now. I'm almost 10 years old, practically grown. Just skip the whole thing."

Mom said patiently, "God answers prayers in his own time, and he decides if it will be a boy or a girl. You will be a big brother to a baby sister or a baby brother sometime around Christmas."

I said, "Are you sure?"

She said, "Yes, I'm sure."

I started praying hard that the new addition would be a baby brother.

Dickie and Charles 1949

Charles Witte arrived in early 1949. I was still puzzled that God waited so long to answer my prayer. I had in mind something like the arrangement that my cousins, Ruth and Patricia, had. They were close in age and had each other to play with and talk to. After we left Beeville, I had only grownups, so I needed God to give me a little brother as a companion and friend.

Charles was special from the start. He was smart like Dad and Grandpa. He occupied Mom and Dad, which gave me a little more freedom to roam around on my Western Flyer. When I moved into my teen years and became interested in girls, Charles became my girl magnet. I already knew that it was hard for me to begin a conversation with anyone, especially girls. Charles could talk to anyone. He roamed around with our dog Buster. The girls loved them both.

The ten-year-age difference was an obstacle. When Charles was 8 years old, I left for the Navy and, in the intervening years, we had little time together. We have always been joined at the heart, and I believe that Charles is the best person I know. He is kind, smart, and family first always. In our old age, we are managing to have some quality time.

Charles – Age 12 – Hunting

LEAVING CUERO

After Charles joined our family, Mom and Dad told me that we were on the move again. We would be leaving Cuero in the middle of the 5th grade, around Christmas, 1949.

I'm not sure why we moved back to Beeville from Cuero. I do know that I missed many things about Cuero then and now. Occasionally, Jerrie and I drive to Cuero and attend Sunday Mass at St. Michael's. I'm always transported to a special time and place. I wonder if my friend Charles is still making folks happy with his music.

4

BEEVILLE, TEXAS

1949 TO 1952

BEEVILLE – SECOND TIME AROUND

In the middle of fifth grade in December 1949, the Witte family was on the move again. I'm not sure why we moved back to Beeville from Cuero. Perhaps Dad was just a restless spirit. We seemed to move about every three years. I do know that Dad and Grandpa Witte had some friction. They often disagreed about money and how Grandpa should run his business. Mom wanted to take my baby brother Charles, who was almost one year old, to Beeville so he could get to know her parents and her brothers and sister. Unfortunately, time does not stand still and this time in Beeville was much different from my first five years when I lived across the street from the Grand Old House. The old house was grand, mostly because it was where Granny and Grandad lived. My cousins Ruth and Patricia and Uncle Billy and Aunt Sue Ellen now lived next door, rather than upstairs in the old house.

Granny and Grandad aged while we were living in Ingleside and Cuero. Time had seemed to be particularly harsh to Grandad, PW

Morrow. I still tagged along with Grandad to the tavern and went with him on painting estimates: however, we no longer lived across the street, and these special times were just that, special times that we both knew were slipping away. Grandad still let me hold his Stetson. I cherished those times because that Stetson was the personification of PW Morrow. If I am going to get a special hat, I'd better do it soon.

Even though I was looking forward to being close to Granny and Grandad and my cousins Ruth, Patricia and Pete, I had bonded with my Cuero family and friends, the Boldt family in Victoria, and St. Michael's church and school.

In Cuero, unless I was in trouble, I had the run of the town on my Western Flyer bicycle. There was something special about the quiet prayerful time in St. Michael's Catholic Church. These days I try a variety of meditation and contemplative prayers but, somehow, I never achieve what seemed to be the genuine connection with God that I experienced as a child in Cuero, Texas. The only other time I experienced this feeling was when I was fishing with my Granny. We always had to be quiet so we would not scare the fish. Granny could have taught monks a lot about contemplation.

In Beeville, in seventh and eighth grade, the process of impending adolescence seemed to overshadow my relations with my family. It was sort of like a preview of what it would be like to be a teenager. I seemed to be more interested in what my school acquaintances thought I should do than what my parents would want me to do. Even more disturbing, I noticed girls differently. Previously, I would dismiss girls as close friends when they did not have an interest in hunting and fishing or even sports. My cousins Ruth and Patricia were girls, but they were like sisters to me. They did not count as the girls I was concerned about.

I was excited about the move to Beeville because it included all the rituals that went with being close to the Beeville family. There were cousins for friends, and we had great times together. I had Granny and Grandad close. I had fried chicken for Sunday dinner. I had chickens to feed. I had quiet time with Granny to replace my visits to St. Michael's Church.

COUSINS

When I returned to Beeville, my cousins Ruth, Patricia, and Pete were at the age that we had the freedom to do many things together, without the supervision of parents. Ruth and Patricia were like big sisters to me.

Cousins Ruth with real Six Shooter, Juanita, Dickie, Patricia, and Pete. Cowboy suits made by Aunt Sue Ellen

Cousins: Patricia Ruth Charles and Dick

We rode horses together, we hunted and fished together, and we shared the problems of growing up. The fact that I attended Catholic School, and Ruth and Patricia attended public school sometimes gave us a different perspective on similar problems.

HUNTING WITH PETE (TWELVE YEARS OLD)

While my cousin Pete and I were not lifelong buddies like I was with Ruth and Patricia, we had several years in Beeville in the early 1950s, when we were great friends.

Pete (left) and Dick, Age 12 - 1950

Dear God,
As always, I thank you for Mom and Dad and my little
brother. God, I especially want to thank you for letting me be
a Texan, with a real hunting gun. I also want to thank you for
letting me have cousins to go hunting with.

Today, my cousin Pete and I went rabbit hunting. Pete told me that this was the day because Old Man Weitzel had moved his

Brahman Bull (Brute) to the south pasture so it would be safe for us to hunt the north pasture, which was our favorite. The north pasture was just a short walk through the woods from Pete's house and he knew that the rabbits were plentiful. There were a lot of Live Oaks in the north pasture for us to sit under to eat our lunch.

I brought an extra fried egg sandwich, bananas, apples, and homemade cookies. Mom said that Pete loved her fried egg sandwiches, and he might not have much in his lunch bag today. She said his mom was stretching a thin dime thinner than it already was these days.

As it turned out, Mom was wrong, at least about the lunch. Pete had a hefty lunch of Granny's fried mashed potato sandwiches which I loved, and I knew Pete would share.

Pete lived out in the country about five miles, and I loved the bicycle ride to his house. I liked the country, but I liked that I lived in a town where I was only a few blocks bike ride to stop by Granny's for a cookie or to see my cousins Ruth and Patricia. God, cousins are one of your best inventions.

I loved Cuero. In Cuero, I got to see Grandpa Witte every day. Everyone said that Grandpa Witte never talked, but he talked to me every day. I learned more from him than I did in school or college. But there were no cousins in Cuero. The closest cousins were 30 miles away in Victoria. I would have loved to ride my bike to Victoria, but Mom said no even before I asked the question. I don't know how moms know what you're thinking.

Anyway, back to hunting with Pete. The rule was that I had to be home by 6:00 p.m. because that was supper time. If you were late for supper at the Witte house, you went to bed without eating. It was not that strict at Granny's house or my cousin's house. But at our house, it was a firm rule. Mom said it was because Granny and Grandad, and my Beeville cousins were Irish American. Dad was a German American, like Grandpa Witte. They liked their rules.

Our family had a general hunting rule: Never Shoot Anything You Don't Intend to Eat. If you take target practice, use a paper target or an empty can, not one of God's creatures. I knew Dad trusted me with my gun. I had been hunting with him for rabbits, squirrels, and deer since I was six, half of my life.

Pete and I got out to the pasture about 9:00 a.m., and immediately bagged a couple of cottontails. There would be meat on the table at Pete's house tonight. Pete said he was tired of beans, and Mom had already told me to leave anything we killed today with Pete.

Pete and I decided on an early lunch under our favorite Live Oak. It was so hot that I swear you could smell the heat. The way we were sweating, I'll bet you could smell us, too. After those fried egg sandwiches and mashed potato sandwiches, we both leaned back and fell asleep.

When I woke up a short time later, we were not alone. I could hear the javelinas rooting, and I could feel my fear. We were surrounded by a pack of five. They had already finished our lunch and by the sound and look of them, they were ready to finish us off. I woke Pete. As a country kid, Pete was tougher than me.

He said, "Just climb the damn tree."

I couldn't believe that my cousin was cussin' but I climbed the tree. Pete said that when the hogs got bored, they would leave. But the hogs didn't leave. They set up camp. Before the day was out, I was cussin' too and scared crazy. In addition to the javelinas, I was sure that before long, the pack of wild dogs that Mr. Weitzel said got one of his cows was going to finish us off.

About 8:00 p.m. I heard a sound that was music to my ears. My uncle's dune-buggy was loose in the pasture. With bright spotlights, I knew we were going to be safe. Those javelinas knew it, too. If those wild dogs were around, they would keep their distance. They knew that anything that sounded like that would have big guns.

Dear God,
Tonight, I doubly thank you, not only for cousins but for uncles and family in general. Thanks to family, I am sleeping in my bed tonight, with my baby brother close enough to touch, and the knowledge that one javelina was not fast enough to escape my uncle's 30-30. That javelina will soon be sausage and perhaps, part of a new batch of hot tamales.

LAW AND ORDER IN BEE COUNTY

Vail Ennis, Bee County Sheriff from 1945-1952, was to me, a real Wild West Sheriff. I secretly called him the Lone Ranger. The Sheriff was often quoted as saying, "I am hell-bent to keep Beeville cleaned up, so a lady can go up the street, day or night."

Most say he was successful in making Bee County and Beeville safe. The complaints against him said that he kept it safe through fear and intimidation. Ennis killed eight men during his tenure as Sheriff and narrowly escaped his death during a bloody shootout, where he took five bullets to his gut and chest before he pulled his Colt.44 revolver and killed his two assailants. When I heard this, I told Dad, "Sheriff Ennis really is the Lone Ranger."

Vail drove a fast car. His Hudson would run 110 miles per hour. According to legend, after taking five bullets in a shoot-out, he pulled his .44 and pointed it at the man who was going to drive him to the hospital. He said, "Put this Hudson at 110 mph, or I'll shoot you too."

Dad and Vail often talked about fast cars. He said Vail would bet $100.00 that he could outrun any production car in Bee County. Dad was sure that the new 1949 Oldsmobile Rocket 88 would run at least 120 mph. But he never challenged Vail to a race.

Vail Ennis was not trained as a lawman. He was an oilfield worker who earned the reputation of being tough. Vail Ennis never walked away from a fight. A Texas Ranger supposedly convinced him that he should officially be on the side of law and order to keep all the hell raisers in check.

In 1944, with his *Never Back Down* reputation, Vail Ennis ran for Sheriff and won by 81 votes. As a kid, I both feared and admired him. I'm glad Dad never challenged him to a race, and I'm glad that Vail Ennis made it possible for all the ladies in my family to walk up the street, day, or night.

Vail Ennis wore a Stetson just like Grandad. They were both the kind of guys that didn't seem completely dressed without their hat. A picture of Vail Ennis, complete with his Stetson, hung in the Bee County Sheriff's Office for many years.

Vail Ennis and his family lived in the Bee County Jail. I always gave the jail a wide berth, yet always hoped to catch a glance of Vail getting into his Hudson. It would have been like watching the Lone Ranger mounting Silver.

ST. JOSEPH'S CATHOLIC SCHOOL

In Beeville, I would attend St. Joseph's Catholic School and it would be a fresh start for me. I became Dick instead of Dickie. David, my sometimes friend was probably right, Dickie was kind of a sissy name. It did not sound sissy when Grandpa called me Herr Dickie. I did my research about names and I found out that Dick, or Dickie, was a nickname for Richard. I also found out there was a Saint Richard, so my baptism wasn't invalid as David had suggested. If I did go to Hell, it would have nothing to do with the name Dickie. I decided that Dick seemed to be better for an older kid and Dick I have remained for most of my life, except for a few sports or work-related nicknames that came along the way.

At St. Joseph's, I continued to be an Altar Boy in church, and I had many new acquaintances in addition to my cousins. A few of these acquaintances were good friends. We even had a football team for the sixth, seventh, and eighth grades at St. Joseph's. Dad was our coach and I loved having him close to me. During football season, Dad and I always got along very well. We were both doing something we loved. I was not a star, but I tried hard and that seemed to impress Dad. He was a great coach. He knew as much about football as he did about automobiles. It was difficult to find teams our size to play, so our opponents were always from much larger schools. Dad taught us that we should evaluate our success on how we played the game and whether we were having fun playing football, rather than the final score.

I remember one game against Beeville Junior High School. My

cousins were in the stands, and it was important to me that we make a good showing. We had just enough players to have one team that played both offense and defense. We had a total of three substitutes. Beeville Junior High School had enough players for two complete teams. We lost the game by one touchdown, but it was a real moral victory for our team. On a personal note, I had a good showing. I blocked a punt and caught a nice pass. My cousins told me I had a good game, and that Dad was a great coach.

Dad was also involved in the Knights of Columbus at St. Joseph's. He let me help in the set-up for all the Knights related events such as Bingo and church cookouts. He told me that someday I could be a Knight and help raise funds for the poor, and all the church projects that the Bishop would never fund, such as our football team and the Boy Scout troop. I'm not sure what he would think of the fact that it took me almost 80 years to become a Knight. He'd probably say something like, "That boy always puts things off."

<hr>

SCOUTING WASHOUT

My Boy Scout experience was short-lived. I fell in with a couple of older boys who found me to be a willing accomplice in their mischief. In Cuero, I might have given one of them a bloody nose for even suggesting that I do something that would embarrass my parents or my cousins. Beeville was a new time for me.

I got kicked out of Boy Scout Summer Camp for being one of the scouts caught blowing up sacks of flour with cherry bombs. The sacks of flour were placed in the Scoutmaster's tent. The tent included the scoutmaster for the troop sponsored by the First Baptist Church in Beeville. This was my cousin's church and had been Mom's church before her conversion to the Catholic faith.

For about six hours after we were nabbed by the scouting police for the crime, and before Dad was summoned to take me home, my two co-conspirators and I had to stay in a roped-off area behind the camp administrator's office. We each had to wear a sign that said, "I

am a nuisance to the camp." I dropped scouting as a Tenderfoot washout. Dad resigned as Assistant Scoutmaster. Thank goodness for my brother Charles. He restored the family's honor in the Scouting world. Charles excelled in all aspects of scouting. I have spent many nights camping, but my camping experience with the Boy Scouts of America was much shorter. The event was as embarrassing for Mom as the kindergarten escape. My teacher, Sister Theresa said that she was ashamed of my behavior.

While fishing, I asked my granny what I should do. She said, "Quiet! You will scare the fish."

While being a camp nuisance gave me a bit of bad-boy notoriety, shaming Mom and Sister Theresa was painful. My cousins were upset with me. They let me know in no uncertain terms that blowing up the tent of the First Baptist Church Scoutmaster was hard to forgive.

WORKING MAN

After dropping scouting, I set my extra time to get a job. We lived just down the street from the HEB Grocery Store. I swept the aisles on Mondays, Wednesdays, and Fridays after school. The floors I swept were wooden. I spread a sawdust mixture on the floor and swept. The floors smelled great after I finished. On Saturdays, I worked at the butcher shop in the IGA Grocery Store. I ground hamburger meat and cleaned the equipment and did anything else they needed. Work kept me out of trouble and it still does.

Work was also good for the Pickle Jar. I wrote Grandpa to tell him how much money I had. He sent me back a note saying, *Be careful, how much you have is not the point. Ask yourself, Did you pay yourself each time you worked?*

GIRLS AND EIGHTH GRADE BOYS

The whole issue of seeing girls in a different light seemed to cause me trouble when I reached eighth grade. I first mentioned this issue to my uncles and Dad when we were on a fishing trip. I said, "I seem to want to be around girls even if they are not interested in hunting, fishing, or sports. I've never had this problem before. What should I do?"

My question was followed by a question from Dad. "What did these girls look like and what did they say when you introduced yourself?" I replied that they were pretty, and I didn't dare to introduce myself. The episode became a joke that my fishing buddies did not keep to themselves.

There was one girl that my friend Fred and I found particularly attractive. She was at least a couple of years older. When she worked in her father's store, she often wore short shorts with a strapless top. Fred and I walked the aisles just to catch a glimpse of her. I named her The Vision. The Vision either did not mind the antics of a couple of young boys, or she was too lazy to run us off.

Sometimes, during this awakening, I crossed the boy-girl barrier. I spoke to one of the pretty girls in my class. Her name for this story is Laura. Laura had a lot of things going for her. She was pretty, and she liked sports. Sports gave me a reason to talk to her. Laura's family owned a small store down the street from the GMC Dealer where Dad worked. I often visited this small dealership and conversed with everyone who worked there. I was always welcome. There was a relaxed atmosphere at this place of business. I am sure there are no dealerships like that today. Everyone was busy but seemed happy. Perhaps they had met the Grandpa Witte Enough is Enough criteria.

I was fascinated with the new Oldsmobiles at that time. The new 1949 Oldsmobile Rocket 88 had the first production overhead-valve V-8 engine in America, and probably the world. The Rocket 88 was an extremely fast car. I decided that I would one day own a fast Oldsmobile. I did eventually own a 1949 Oldsmobile Rocket 88. I also owned a 1953 Oldsmobile convertible and I owned the last real Oldsmobile, the Oldsmobile Tornado. Who says that kids need to grow up? After the Tornado, the Oldsmobile became a tank, and the brand disappeared from the landscape.

The Rialto, Beeville

Back to Laura, the first pretty girl that I dared to speak to. Mom would say thank goodness he let cars distract him from adolescent impulses. After I visited the car dealership, I would walk down to Laura's shop where we would have a cookie and visit. I got the feeling that Laura's mom liked me.

I eventually got up the courage to ask Laura to a Saturday matinee at the Rialto Theater in Beeville. It was an easy walk. Using my work money, I could afford both tickets and still have money for snacks. Laura said she had to watch her waistline, so she only wanted a Coke. Laura was an inexpensive date.

About the third Saturday matinee, I got the courage to put my arm around Laura's shoulder and I even attempted a peck on her cheek. A spying cousin saw the entire episode. It was just like scout camp. Mom knew the sordid details by nightfall. I clearly could not be trusted to take a girl to the Saturday matinee at the Rialto.

Laura and I had a friendship that survived. We eventually went back to the Rialto. We decided to be friends without any romantic stuff until we were older. My friendship with Laura was different than my friendship with guys, but she was a friend indeed. I liked having a friend who was a girl.

I hope Laura had a great life because she was a great friend. She made it possible for me to have many friends that were girls in my life. Thank you, Laura.

The Shorty Incident

I always felt that the Shorty Incident was Dad's way of getting even for the scouting episode. A friend of Dad gave me a fighting gamecock. I named him Shorty. Shorty was a beautiful chicken with bright red and green feathers, but he was born with one leg shorter than the other. So, he became my pet rather than a fighting gamecock.

I never equated fighting gamecocks with something cruel. I never saw a chicken fight. Dad said it was just something that folks did for entertainment. I was glad Shorty did not need to fight another chicken.

Shorty got along with Granny's chickens. Shorty got along with everyone except Dad. Shorty and Herbert ruffled each other's feathers. On occasion, Shorty would go into attack mode and go after Dad with his long sharp claws. When Dad was relaxed and having his evening Lone Star beer, Shorty would attack. I had been told to take Shorty to get his claws trimmed so that he would be safe around people. I never got around to the task. One night I came home after the Saturday matinee at the Rialto and we had chicken salad for supper. I loved Mom's chicken salad sandwiches. It was not until the next day, after church, that I discovered that Shorty was missing.

Grandad reported that the final confrontation between Shorty and Dad had been a close battle. But in the end, Shorty was a real fighting gamecock. He gave his life for the joy of the fight.

I hardly spoke to Dad for weeks. I finally resolved that Shorty was not much different than Granny's Rhode Island Reds and White Leghorns. They had to give their lives each week for Sunday dinner and sometimes by my hand. I was glad I was not a chicken, and particularly, not a pet chicken. Their fate always seemed to be the same as the other chickens. They ended up on a plate. Still, I did not speak to Dad for quite a while.

Dad finally extended a peace offering. He was a magician with cars. Cars were something we agreed on. We both loved cars. Dad spent over a year restoring a 1940 Ford coupe. Those who had seen the coupe in the shop envied it. The car was a black beauty. When Dad asked if I would like to take one of the first rides in the coupe, I cried.

I thought I may have even seen a tear shed by Dad. I can still hear that flathead V-8 engine. The coupe was more beautiful than the day it rolled off the showroom floor. Shorty was forgiven but never forgotten. I know there are two sides to every story. Perhaps in the next reality, Shorty and Dad can each tell their side of this family tragedy.

THE DRAGLINE TWINS

One of our neighbors in Beeville ran a land clearing business. Most of his work was in the scrub brush of Bee County and surrounding areas. He used a dragline to clear the land. The dragline was a huge chain, stretched between two bulldozers. The chain was dragged across the land and cleared the land of all but the largest trees. The trees that were left standing depended on the desires of the landowner. On this occasion, one of the dozers backed into a large Live Oak that was to be left on the property. It did not hurt the tree but later when the workers were taking their break under the shade of the tree, they found two baby squirrels. The mother squirrel was nowhere to be found and the babies barely had their eyes open.

Our neighbor said, "I'll take these babies home to the neighbor kid. He already has a fighting gamecock for a pet, and the squirrels could give the chicken something to chase."

I called my new pets the Dragline Twins.

My cousins Ruth and Patricia had given me a couple of pet squirrels and their dad, my Uncle Billy, had built them a running wheel so we were set for more squirrels. We fed the twins with a baby bottle from a veterinary friend of Dad. (Good car mechanics always had lots of friends.) My squirrels were the only pets Dad seemed happy with. I think he liked the fact that they could look after themselves. Yet they were still our pets.

The twins, which we called Henry and Harriet, would sit beside me, and let me feed them. They would let Shorty, my gamecock, chase them but never catch them. Later, after we got our dog, Buster, they let Buster chase them. They all seemed to know that they lived together and played together at our house in Beeville, with the huge oak tree in the back yard. If that tree is still standing, I'm sure the descendants of the Dragline Twins reside there and enjoy the endless supply of acorns provided by the oak tree.

BUSTER – THE HOUND DOG WHO WASN'T

I thought the opportunity for a free hunting dog was what I needed to get Dad to let me have another dog. When it appeared that I could get a genuine working hound dog, for free, Dad was sold. I worked at St. Joseph's School Cafeteria as one of my sidelines. The lady who ran the cafeteria was one of my favorite people in the world. She was like Granny except much younger. She never stopped working, yet she always seemed to be happy. Her son was one of my best friends. His dog, Mildred, was a great hunting dog. Mildred was with child. Mildred had been with another hunting dog, a Red Bone Hound. There were great expectations for Mildred's litter. I had been promised one of Mildred's puppies and I was sure that any dog that was a combination of Mildred and a Red Bone Hound would elevate my hunting to the next level.

The litter was a big surprise. None of the puppies looked anything like the classic Red Bone Hound. Taking Dad's advice, I chose the first male that would choose me. Buster, which sounded like a hound dog name to me, came to me every time I visited the litter.

| Nannie Lee and Buster

By the time he came home with me, we were soul mates. Buster was never a hunting dog, but he was one of my best friends. Buster shared his love with my brother Charles. Despite our 10-year age difference, Buster loved both me and my brother, Charles. Buster loved everyone in the family, and I think everyone loved him.

Jerrie and Buster

Charles and Buster

Buster was the last family pet of my childhood and even though he never caught a rabbit, he did capture a lot of hearts. I can still picture my little brother, at about age six, racing down the street on his bicycle, with Buster in his basket. At every stop, Buster would get his ears scratched by whoever Charles stopped to visit. Buster was a free spirit. He was never fenced in, yet there never was a complaint from anyone.

Buster was a survivor. While he never chased another animal other than for fun, he hated snakes. Buster kept our yard clear of snakes, which was hard to do when you lived in South Texas. One big rattler thought he had taken care of Buster. But Buster survived. He swelled till he seemed to be twice his normal size, and then, with what we thought were his final days, Mom said, "We just petted him back to life."

After that episode Buster was fearless. The snakes seemed to believe they were invincible and kept their distance. I loved the runt of Mildred's litter.

Madonna and Buster

While I had many dogs in my lifetime, I only had one other dog that came close to occupying as much space in my heart as Buster. Bartholomew Dias (Bart) our black and tan Dachshund was named for a Portuguese explorer (1450-1500). The explorer was studied by my daughter Sarah to such an extent that he became part of the family. We kept Bartholomew in the family by naming our new dog for him. Bart was about the size of Buster with the same face but with shorter legs. I believe Mildred made friends with a Dachshund in addition to the Red Bone Hound. Buster had the same soulful eyes as our Bart. These days, I am thankful to be dogless, with only good memories of a few dear friends.

BEEVILLE HOME

We did not own our own home in Beeville. The last house we rented in Beeville was one of the homes I remember most fondly for our family. Mom loved this house. The house was larger than any other home I lived in as a child. I could ride my bike or walk almost anywhere I needed to go from this house. One of the things I loved about the house was the big backyard with a huge oak tree. The back yard was home to all my pets, my squirrels, my gamecock, and my dog. Most of the major events in this chapter occurred while we lived in this house. The exception was the scouting fiasco. During that time, we lived in a converted washateria. As Mom would say, it was good to put both the washateria and the scouting episode behind us.

THE GREAT BLACK-EYED PEA INCIDENT

About halfway through the first semester of eighth grade, I learned that we were moving again. Dad had decided that it was time for him to leave the automotive business. Without the rest of us knowing, he had been quietly teaching himself accounting and decided he was going to go into the life insurance business.

A major social event occurred when Dad invited his prospective new boss to our house for dinner. Mom was excited. This was the first time we had lived in a house that had a nice big dining room. I promised to be on my best behavior. My little brother was only about three years old and everybody was concerned that he might be a problem. Charles was not the problem.

About halfway through dinner, the new boss asked if I would pass him the black-eyed peas. As I passed them, the bowl slipped out of my hands and ended in the lap of the new boss. Mom was mortified. The new boss was in shock. Dad just shook his head. Charles thought the whole thing was hilarious and he saved the day. His spontaneous laughter was infectious and soon everybody at the table was laughing, except Mom. Mom was crying.

Dad got the job and the new boss became a family friend. I was reminded about the incident forever. Dad's new job set the stage for the last chapter of my childhood.

LIFE WITH UNCLE GENE AND AUNT ALENE

When the family moved fifty miles from Beeville to Ingleside for Dad to take his new job, my parents let me stay with Uncle Gene and Aunt Alene to complete the fall semester of eighth grade at St. Joseph's, in Beeville. Uncle Gene was Mom's younger brother. I loved being around Gene and Alene.

Uncle Gene and Aunt Alene

They were closer to my age than any of the other relatives from my parent's generation. They did not treat me like a child. The first night at their house, we had a nice meal with meat, vegetables, and iced tea. There were no mashed potatoes and gravy. The meal was great, and we had plenty to eat without mashed potatoes. I had this fear that Alene had cooked mashed potatoes and gravy and forgotten to serve them. She had this wonderful Chambers Range with lots of hiding places. I was concerned that she would be embarrassed for forgetting to serve the potatoes.

I finally said, "I think you forgot the mashed potatoes and gravy."

Alene knew that at my house we had mashed potatoes and gravy every night, except Fridays. On Friday, we either had fried fish with pinto beans, coleslaw, and skillet fried potatoes or pinto beans and cornbread.

Alene and Gene broke out laughing. They wondered how long it would take for me to notice the missing potatoes. The meal was a way for them to explain that when they were in their own house, they ate and cooked differently than the extended family. They were into health before it was popular to do such a thing. I was always excited to eat with them and my embarrassing question remained private between us. Uncle Gene was a lifelong role model for me. In his thirties, he sold his successful business and moved to San Marcos, Texas to pursue a college degree at Southwest Texas State College (now Texas State University) on his G.I. Bill.

Uncle Gene and Aunt Alene

The semester I stayed with Alene and Gene remains a high point of my childhood. In addition to experiencing new food choices, Gene taught me how to sand and finish wood floors, install floor tile and sell paint and painting supplies. Gene also taught me how to drive his truck which served me well when I moved to Ingleside. I would follow in the footsteps of Uncle Gene by joining the U.S. Navy and then attending college as an adult.

5

INGLESIDE, TEXAS

1952-1957

INGLESIDE OR SINTON – THE BIG DECISION

Dad's new job was centered in Sinton Texas. Dad's territory also covered Ingleside, and Aransas Pass, so they were both possibilities for our new home. I lived in Ingleside during the latter part of World War II and immediately after the war.

CONSIDERATIONS FROM THE 1940's INGLESIDE EXPERIENCE

The first time we lived in Ingleside was a traumatic time of family separation for me and Mom and a time for difficult decisions for Dad. It was also a time that included peak experiences that helped define my future.

School experiences were significant. My kindergarten behavior resulted in me being expelled. The next year I had a positive and special experience with an exceptional first-grade teacher.

My first hurricane gave me insight into Dad. That hurricane

experience also let me know that danger and excitement were linked. The link between danger and excitement makes life exciting.

My first non-cousin friend opened my eyes to the fact that cousins were not the only friends I could have. I could have friends and cousins. In Ingleside, I had my first grandfather figure that was not kinfolks. That period in Ingleside was the first time Mom was away from her parents and her new friends became like family. After Ingleside in the 1940s, Mom and I both had a new definition of family. We knew that friends sometimes became family.

Out of my early experiences in Ingleside, I learned several things about myself.

1. I did not have a fear of school. I had a fear of failure. While the fear of failure remains, I have learned that fear is not always negative. Fear can give me an edge and help me be successful. I learned to accept that failure is going to happen and when it does happen, it will likely be an excellent teacher.

2. Dangers often bring out our best. Responding to danger can be exciting and rewarding and usually has unexpected consequences. During my first hurricane in Ingleside, Dad was busy responding to needs for assistance at the refinery and in the community. I could tell that he was tired, but he took the time to show me some of the storm damage and why we needed to respect Mother Nature. I could tell he was in a high energy mode. Responding to that hurricane was a high point for Dad. I knew at that moment that if Dad had gone into the service, he would have quietly done heroic things.

3. Some consequences of the hurricane were special to me. Dad was helping clean up the neighborhood after the hurricane when he decided to make me a canoe out a piece of tin that had blown of a roof. That canoe was the best present I ever received (not counting my Western Flyer bicycle.) Within hours, Dad was the neighborhood canoe builder and we had an armada of canoes that my new friends and I loved. Dad was smiling for the first time in several days. Thank goodness for danger and unexpected

consequences. Dangerous events have contributed to a life worth living for many folks, including me.

4. The family includes friends and the creatures God sends to us for our care. Family and the love of family is the most rewarding of life's treasures and on occasion, it is life's greatest challenge.

I fondly remember the first time I lived in Ingleside, from kindergarten through first grade, and the valuable lessons I learned.

CONSIDERATIONS IN 1952 - SINTON NEVER HAD A CHANCE

My family was trying to decide if our new home would be Sinton or Ingleside. I hoped Ingleside would be the choice. I wanted to be an Ingleside Mustang. I wanted to play football for Emory Bellard. I believed I would find another new friend in Ingleside. I would be without cousins again.

There was considerable discussion on where to move for the new job. I was not sure if I had any input in the final decision, but I let everyone know that I voted for Ingleside. As hard as moving and making new friends was for me, I thought I would have a head start in Ingleside. I heard Dad talking about how great the fishing was in the Ingleside and Aransas Pass area. Dad said that Port Aransas was close for weekend camping, hunting, and fishing. Then, there was football, which seemed to be a strong mutual interest for me and Dad. We both thought that football at Ingleside High School looked promising.

Ingleside, according to the area newspapers, had a new head football coach who had established a promising record in his first year and had most of his starters returning for next year. The coach's name was Emory Bellard, and he was a local boy. Emory grew up in Port Aransas and played football in Aransas Pass. Emory played football in college at the University of Texas. Based on my early experiences in Ingleside, and my football aspirations, I voted for Ingleside to be our new home.

I figured that Dad might vote for Ingleside for the fishing. Dad had many interests, but at this time in his life, he loved to fish and particularly to wade and fish for speckled trout and redfish. Dad was an acknowledged expert fishing for catfish in the Guadalupe River, but he said, "I need excitement, the trout and redfish fight like little ponies." There was not a better place in the world to wade and fish for speckled trout and redfish than Old Ingleside, which was between Ingleside and Aransas Pass.

During discussions about the location of our new home, I heard Mom mention that Sinton was a nice town. Mom was not very assertive and my little brother, Charles, seemed to be up for any adventure. I suspected that Dad's vote would be the vote that counted. I never heard anyone mention Aransas Pass and I am not sure why. Ingleside was the winner and I was glad then, and I'm glad now.

Ingleside was never much to look at, but for most of my adult life, when someone asked me where home was, I would say, Ingleside, Texas. When they asked, "Where in the world is Ingleside, Texas?" I would say, "Ingleside, Texas is Heaven on Earth and is just across the bay from Corpus Christi, Texas."

SALTWATER

I think I have a saltwater gene. I think I inherited that gene from Dad. In Ingleside, I realized that both Dad and I needed to be near saltwater or where we could get to saltwater quickly. In pitching Ingleside as our new home, Dad highlighted wading to fish for speckled trout and redfish. He also highlighted Port Aransas as a great place for hunting, fishing, and camping outings. Dad's sales pitch was true.

During the 1950s, while I became a teenager and survived, the saltwater environment became a part of who I am. I did not love fishing the way Dad did, but I loved being on or near the saltwater of the bays and the Gulf of Mexico.

Sometimes, I enjoyed being on the saltwater alone, or with a partner like Dad or Granny. At other times I enjoyed the loud family and friend gatherings and camping trips at the beach. I moved on after Ingleside to spend time on or under virtually every ocean of the world. I get uncomfortable when I get too far away from saltwater. I don't qualify as an Old Salt, but I am working on it.

Thanks to Dad, and Ingleside, for letting me know that I should not live too far away from the saltwater.

WADE FISHING AT OLD INGLESIDE

Dad taught me how to wade and fish for speckled trout and redfish and I loved it. I loved it for slightly different reasons than Dad. Herbert Witte loved the competition he had with the fish, as he developed his skills in selecting and designing his artificial baits. I remember him designing lures using the latest buck-tail and homemade spoons and other inventions he was sure the fish would love.

If I were along, he would always cast for fresh shrimp. Shrimp seemed to be the only bait I was successful with. The lure of fishing for me was being close to Dad or a friend and being in a quiet and beautiful place on the bay or Gulf of Mexico. I loved everything about the bay at Old Ingleside, including that special smell that some consider offensive. I loved checking in with Mrs. Lee at Lee's Bait Stand. I loved everything about where we lived. The place we waded and fished for speckled trout and redfish is one of those special places that my mind transports me to experience gratitude for life's treasures. My brother Charles became as good at fishing as Dad. I'm certain that neither Dad nor Charles loved the saltwater as much as I do.

PORT ARANSAS – CAMPING

Dad was correct about Port Aransas when deciding on Ingleside. But it was the Port Aransas of a different day. There were no crowds in the

1950s. We would drive over on Friday after work and set up a campsite on the beach. We set camp above the projected high tide mark. Sometimes it would be just our family but usually, we would go with another family and friends.

The typical group would include my Beeville aunts, uncles and cousins, and family friends from Beeville or Dad's work. We usually did not have tents or even chairs except for folding canvas stools. We had folding card tables that served the dual purpose of meal preparation and for card and domino games. No one seemed to care that our campsite was primitive. We tied tarps to poles and to the cars, pickup trucks, and station wagons to create space shaded from direct sun. We had Army-style cots. We brought food for "sandpit" cooking and we also cooked on Coleman stoves that were set up on the tailgate of a station wagon. The back of the station wagon became a kitchen, with a stove and the area behind the stove serving as the kitchen cabinet. We always had bacon, eggs, beans, onions, potatoes, and other staples needed for grilling, frying, and for making a seafood chowder that we never had at home, but that I loved. Even though they were heavy, we used iron skillets for our beach cooking, and my family still prefers iron skillets.

I know that I only remember the good parts and not all the work that made these trips successful. I loved camping and cooking directly on the beach. We slept everywhere, including in the cars and on the beach wrapped in a blanket or a sleeping bag. Sometimes we would have as many as 20 people that would gather at our beach camp. The social informality we did not have at home was special. The beach seemed to loosen spirits. I know that alcohol was a lubricant for a few of the adults, but I never saw anyone have over a few beers. The informal atmosphere contributed to an adolescent experience that I never shared before this writing.

During the summer before my freshman year in high school, I was running out of the dunes on my way back to the beach, when I encountered a very pretty lady from our group. She was not one of my relatives and she was stark naked, behind a car, changing into her bathing suit. After we both recovered, she smiled and turned her back to me and continued dressing. I ran as fast as I could to the beach and straight into the Gulf of Mexico. I never told a soul about this experience. I probably should have had some profound insight. Instead, I remember thinking, "So this is what they look like" then a short prayer escaped my lips, "God please do not let this lady tell anyone."

The pretty lady never said a word to me, but I swear she smiled at me in a way that made me blush for the rest of the day. Considering the way gossip works, I don't think she ever told anyone.

Once we were home, I never saw that special beach smile again. If she is still around, she would be close to ninety years old. I hope she will not mind me sharing this story.

PORT ARANSAS – TARPON FISHING

Another favorite Port Aransas adventure was watching the tarpon fishermen, at the tarpon hole, at the end of the pier. I remember thinking, "I'll bet that both the tarpon and the tarpon fishermen love this game." That is why they both keep coming back. Dad said, "We don't eat tarpon, so we don't fish for tarpon." I wondered if there was some other reason, like perhaps money, that Dad didn't participate in tarpon fishing or other big game fishing that was available just offshore.

PORT ARANSAS – HUNTING FROM THE DUNES

An activity with my uncles was hunting from the dunes. I did not shoot; I was the bird dog. I would run out of the dunes, sometimes into the Gulf of Mexico, to retrieve the birds. It was great fun, and I was in great shape. I would give almost anything for some of that energy, these days.

FLOUNDER FISHING WITH UNCLES

I rolled into my usual parking spot at home on Humble Street in Ingleside Texas about 10:00 pm on a Friday. I racked my mufflers a couple of times to let my dog, Buster, know I was home. Buster would need to move because he slept where I parked my car and would need a wake-up call. The mufflers would let my parents know that I was home. Since I was currently sleeping in my loft in the garage, I didn't always go into the house when I got home from teenage socializing. Tonight was different. My uncles from Beeville were here to go flounder fishing, and I was going with them.

Flounder was my favorite fish. Everyone else in the family preferred speckled trout and redfish. Today, when I look forward to my visits to "Bob's Catfish 'n More" in Georgetown, Texas, I appreciate the catfish but I am reminded of the time when I could choose between several kinds of fresh fish every week.

I'd already had a great evening dancing with my steady girl, Jerrie Swinney, at the Ingleside Youth Center. Jerrie understood my excitement to get home early because going fishing with family was also a big event at her house. Jerrie's dad, Earl, was the real fisherman in her family. Uncle Bubba was the official family fish storyteller and her Uncle Marvin and Aunt Dotta spent every minute they could fishing together as a family. Jerrie loved fishing. She preferred pier fishing on the Sun Pipeline docks to early morning wading adventures like I would participate in with my uncles.

As I walked into the house, I saw that Uncle Billy, Uncle Gene, Mom, and Dad were still playing 42, their favorite domino game. They were paired up with Uncle Billy and Mom as partners. Billy was a serious player and Mom followed his strategy. Dad, the other serious player, was paired with Uncle Gene. Gene was a good player, but dominos was just a game to him. I always had the feeling that Gene and Mom played mostly for the socializing, and Dad and Billy played for the competition. They were all having a great time.

Billy looked up from his hand and said, "Well, Fat Boy, you have time for a nap, but we'll be leaving at 2:00 a.m. sharp. The car is loaded, and we'll not be waiting around."

I noticed Mom's disapproving glance at the Fat Boy comment. I didn't care. I was beefed up for football. The other person who called me Fat Boy was Jerrie's dad. I had the feeling that Earl and Uncle Billy weren't being hurtful. They didn't agree with my beefing up plan, and thought I needed a reminder.

I ignored the comment and said, "I'm the one who gets up early every morning to roll newspapers. You old guys will not be waiting on me."

Mom gave another disapproving look.

I was excited about the flounder trip. This was one of my favorite activities and was a real family gift. Mom and Dad would be getting up at 4:00 a.m. to run my paper route so I could be with my uncles.

Since we moved back to Ingleside, I missed being with my uncles and I

Uncle Billy and Uncle Gene in uniforms

believe they missed spending time with me. They treated me as if they enjoyed teaching me new skills. I learned all kinds of things from my uncles, from trim painting a window, to sanding hardwood floors, to learning how to drive a pick-up, and for this trip, I would gain experience in flounder fishing.

We left Ingleside before 2:00 am. We were all excited to be on the road. We headed toward the ferry landing at Port Aransas. Our destination was a spot along the bay flats before the ferry landing. This was my uncles' special spot.

Billy said that he needed still water that was about halfway between knee-deep and a wet butt. I would walk between Billy and Gene and carry a Coleman Lantern. The lantern would cast enough light for my uncles to see flounder and distinguish them from the occasional stingray, as they both snuggled on the sandy bottom.

While we each had a long stringer attached to our waist, most of the flounder would end up on the stringer of the lantern carrier. When

I asked about the length of the stringer, I was told that it was long so that if a shark attacked our catch, they would only get our flounder and not us. I had never seen a shark in the flats other than a few small hammerheads, but I never questioned the wisdom of my uncles.

We did not fish for flounder with a fishing pole. If you caught a flounder with a regular fishing pole in those days, it was considered good luck. My uncles were each armed with gigs. Each gig had two sharp prongs that were about ten to twelve inches long, mounted on a round pole that was about four to five feet long and about one inch in diameter. I believe that Dad made the gigs we used but there were plenty of similar commercial gigs on the market. Using the light from the lantern, my uncles would spot flounder as we walked slowly along, with me in the middle. They would gig the flounder and slip the flounder from the gig to the stringer in a smooth motion.

I asked myself, "How did these house painters develop such skills?" My Uncle Billy could paint the trim of a very intricate window with no tools other than his trim brush.

When I asked him how, he said, "I'm an artist. I just paint house trim rather than faces, trees, or a landscape."

Billy was also an artist with a flounder gig. When we had enough flounder, my uncles insisted that I move to one of the gig positions for my lessons in using the gig to catch flounder. They knew I would prefer carrying the lantern, but they also knew that flounder was my favorite fish. What I loved was whole pan-fried small flounder with skillet fries, pinto beans, and coleslaw.

Lured by the promise that I could keep all the flounder I managed to get on the stringer in addition to my family's one-third of the catch, my lessons began. I was not as smooth as my uncles, but I learned. This lesson had to be completed before we could clean up and go to the Bakery Café in Aransas Pass for eggs over easy, a short stack and fried potatoes, bacon or ham, and coffee on our way back home to Ingleside.

In the 1950s, flounder seemed plentiful and fishermen who got on the water at 2:00 a.m. were relatively few. The rules were simple: Don't take more than you or your family and friends can eat before you come back.

Before I was as tall as my uncles, they let me and my cousins, Ruth and Patricia, go flounder fishing with them. We had to go slow because we were short, and we had to hold the lantern high. We traded places often because it was hard work for little folks. My Uncle Gene said, "Slow is good; we're here for the fun." I think Gene practiced 'slow is good' most of his life. Flounder fishing with my uncles was good for my soul and the flounder was also good.

(Just wait till you try my recipes for skillet fries and pan-fried flounder at the end of the book.) I'd better go pack the car. I'm feeling the need for a sand and saltwater fix. I'm close enough that in a short amount of time, I can be on a quiet beach, with my bare toes in the sand and the saltwater. If I look closely, I might see a flounder snuggled quietly in the sand.

INGLESIDE – SETTLING IN

When we moved back to Ingleside, I guessed that someone from my first two years in Ingleside would assist me in adapting to my fourth move as a kid. I never guessed that it would be another adult. Harry, who had been like a substitute grandfather to me in Ingleside after my kindergarten escape, again came to my rescue. Harry owned the hotel and a variety of other rental properties in Ingleside and lived in the hotel. Harry rented the little house behind the hotel to Mom and Dad when they returned to Ingleside in October 1952. Mom and Dad moved to Ingleside with my brother Charles, while I stayed with Aunt Alene and Uncle Gene to complete the first semester of eighth grade.

When I arrived in Ingleside for the second semester of eighth grade, I didn't know Ingleside would be my final childhood home, but I hoped it would be. Harry's rental house was not our final Ingleside home, but it was home to many positive and negative family experiences.

Harry was glad to see me when I joined the family for Christmas in 1952. I'd changed from first grade to eighth grade, but Harry looked the same and treated me as if I had only been gone for a month.

When Harry found out that I had worked at a butcher shop in Beeville, his eyes lit up. Harry raised rabbits that he marketed locally. Harry was unable to get the help he needed to keep up with the demand for fresh rabbits. He needed a helper who could clean the rabbit hutches, muck out under the hutches, and take the rabbit droppings and work them into the ground at the garden plot. He also needed a helper to kill and butcher the rabbits and pack them on ice. I was up for everything except the killing of the rabbits. I told Harry that it would be like killing pets.

Harry said, "If you can eat the chicken you helped to catch for Sunday dinner in Beeville, you can do this. It is just how it is. If we eat meat, we need to learn to process animals humanely. I'll teach you how to do that. The breeding stock is treated as pets, and the rest of the rabbits we treat well until it's time for them to feed us." Harry made it clear that his job offer was an All or None proposition.

Harry did teach me. I learned to appreciate the work and the way we took care of the rabbits. I often thought about Shorty, my gamecock, and how he became chicken salad. I thought about the fact that I only chased white chickens when we chased down a chicken for Sunday dinner in Beeville. I thought about the cottontail rabbits and the squirrels I shot hunting. I was glad I was not a chicken or a rabbit, or a squirrel, but I knew Harry was right. It is just how it is. Harry allowed me to continue to develop work skills and my appreciation for the world of work. I learned that hard decisions are involved in earning a living. If I wanted to work for Harry, I needed to accept that I had to butcher rabbits.

When Harry found out that my Uncle Gene taught me how to drive his pickup truck, I was soon running errands in Harry's old Dodge truck. Harry didn't seem concerned that I didn't have a driver's license. I loved driving his truck. There is nothing better than being behind the wheel of a good truck, with a full tank of gas.

New Friends

Our neighbors at our first house in Ingleside let me know what to expect as I attempted to make new friends in Ingleside. I met Aaron and Darrell and we quickly became friends. Aaron and I both had little brothers and our moms were already friends. Darrell lived just down the street.

Darrell and I were both excited about playing football. I was one grade ahead of Darrell so I would get the first try at football. Darrell and I played football together for three years and I believe we both enjoyed our time as teammates and as Ingleside Mustangs.

By the time school started in January, I had an Ingleside network. I was working for Harry and I had two good friends, Darrell and Aaron. I was no longer a stranger in a new town.

There seemed to be a general laid-back atmosphere in Ingleside even among the downtown merchants. I loved the feeling I had in Ingleside. Ingleside was going to be home. In some ways, Ingleside is still home.

The Accident

Life was not easy at the little house behind the hotel. Dad was on the road much of the time as he developed his new job. The little house was tiny compared to our home in Beeville. A bad family accident occurred while we lived in our house behind the hotel. I believe the small size of the house and kitchen contributed to the accident.

The scene, as described by Mom, began in the kitchen with a large pot of boiling water. As she removed the pot, my little brother, Charles, ran into the kitchen to give her a hug around her legs. The boiling water poured over my brother's back. Charles and Mom were both scarred that day but in different ways.

After the accident, I prayed that we would get a larger and safer house. I wanted a kitchen for Mom that could be her empire. I finally realized that accidents just happen. At our nice big home in Beeville, I poured black-eyed peas in the lap of Dad's new boss while we were all trying to be on our best behavior.

Charles' good humor, after he recovered from his accident, combined with his outgoing personality, served him well. Everyone within striking distance of the little house behind the hotel knew and loved Charles, and he knew no strangers. The hotel was on the main street of the small downtown of Ingleside. Charles was welcome at every business, except the Buckhorn Saloon.

The Buckhorn was still in operation the last time I checked. It was a combined bar and pool hall and was an escape and refuge for its customers. I am sure that PW Morrow would have been a regular at the Buckhorn if he had lived in Ingleside. Charles was a precocious preschooler and was not as welcome at the Buckhorn as he was at the Red & White Grocery, Ramey's Drugstore, the Post Office, Stewart's Pharmacy, or Tommy's IGA Grocery. The kids all liked Jack Clark's Humble station, where an air station was set up for kids to keep the air in their bike tires.

One of Mom's favorite stories about Charles, while we were at the little house behind the hotel, was shared by Aaron's mom. She said that Charles and Buster came over to her house and asked if they could come in and rest because they could not go home. When she asked why, Charles related that, "Mom has some man in the house and told me I had to stay outside till he was gone." Aaron's mom gave Charles a cookie and called Mom. Mom was with Uncle Billy, her brother. Billy had driven over from Beeville to discuss some issues related to their parents.

We stayed at the little house behind the hotel until Dad decided to build our new house. The new house was home for my family until I was grown and gone. Life happened while we lived behind the hotel. I will never forget the lessons learned, friendships made, and Charles' accident.

My friends Aaron and Darrell both became pilots while I chose to go in the opposite direction, as a submarine sailor. Aaron gave his life as a Navy pilot.

When we moved from the rental house, I began to lose touch with

Harry. Harry was a true friend and was like family. Harry's contribution to legal driving is described below.

HARRY AND DRIVING

I came stumbling out of the little house behind the hotel one Saturday morning, and Harry said, "Dick, I thought I told you to take that load of trash to the dump. I'll be going to Corpus tomorrow. If I need to go to the dump before I go, I'm going to dock your pay."

Money always got my attention. I washed my face, jumped into the truck, and headed for the dump. As I drove off, I thought I saw Harry and Dad laughing.

When I got to the dump, the Constable was there and walked over to the truck and said, "Let me see your Driver's License."

I said, "I don't have one. I didn't think you needed one to drive to the dump."

The Constable said, "Well, show me your Learner's Permit."

I said, "I don't have that either."

The Constable said, "Well, boy, you are in *Big Trouble* and so is your Daddy and Harry down at the Hotel."

I said, "What am I going to do?"

He said, "You are going to drive that truck home so Harry can go to Corpus, and then you are going to get your Daddy to sign the paper saying you need to drive, at fourteen, so you can work and help your family. Then, you are going to sign up for Leon Taylor's Driver's Education Class as soon as you are able. If you don't pass the class, I'm going to throw you in jail for driving without a license and endangering the good folks of Ingleside."

When I got back to the hotel, Dad and Harry were sitting at a picnic table, drinking coffee. I knew the fix was in when Dad handed me the paper I needed. The form said I needed to drive before the normal age because of family necessity. The three of them had decided that it was time for me to become legal.

Leon Taylor was not surprised when I signed up for his class in my freshman year. I'm not sure that those four solid citizens of Ingleside realized the danger they were about to unleash on the population when I became legal to drive. What a place to grow up. There were parents everywhere.

DRIVER'S EDUCATION

With driving lessons from my Uncle Gene, plus practice driving to the dump for Harry, I was sure I was ready for legal driving. I took Driver's Education with the Ingleside High School Principal, Leon Taylor. The car used in the class was a 1953 six-cylinder Ford with a standard shift. I was sure that I didn't need the class to pass my driver's test because I was already a great driver. While I had only driven in the field across from my Uncle Gene's house in Beeville and from the hotel to the dump in Ingleside, how difficult could it be to drive on the highway to Aransas Pass where we would practice parallel parking and take our driver's test?

There were good reasons to take the class that had nothing to do with driving skill. Primary among the reasons to take the class was a discount on car insurance. Dad's rule was clear. If you want to drive, you pay the additional car insurance. Driver's Education was my path to saving money. Drivers Education should be an easy class, or so I thought.

Leon Taylor taught me a lot about driving and the safety rules that would be on the driver's test and that would help me be a safe driver. I probably did not tell Leon or anyone else what a great class Driver's Education was. It would not have been cool to tell anyone you needed a class to be a good driver. All male Texans were born knowing how to ride a horse, drive a fast car, and keep our boots somewhere between scuffed and the perfect shine.

Although I was a great driver, I couldn't parallel park. I was nervous driving in the big city of Aransas Pass, and I was afraid to pass on the highway driving to Aransas Pass. Driving in Aransas Pass in the

1950s was much different than driving in Ingleside from the hotel to the dump.

I am forever grateful for the conspiracy of Dad, Harry, and our Constable to get me into Driver's Education early in my high school adventure. I am also thankful that Leon was a patient man. He taught us real driving skills and he gave us simple rules. I passed the driver's test the first time with no problems.

Leon's knowledge of teenagers and driving made him an exceptional teacher. He taught me that driving was serious business. I believe I became a safe driver although not a quiet driver. Over the next four years, I was glad that I had the opportunity to get to know Leon well when I was a freshman and that he became acquainted with me early in my time at Ingleside High School.

After getting my Driver's License, the next step to driving a car was to go through an interview and grilling by Mrs. Robinson, the insurance lady. She told me, "If you are not a responsible driver, you could ruin the insurance rating for your entire family and jeopardize ever getting car insurance when you are an adult."

My children had to go through this same lecture when it was time for them to start driving. Some lessons simply must be passed to the next generation.

AUTOMOBILES – 1948 FORD

The next major hurdle was that I would need a car to drive. Dad needed the family car for his work. I began to think that perhaps I should just borrow Harry's truck as he was not as strict about following rules. In my heart, I already knew that would be a short-term solution.

Dad purchased a 1948 Ford. The Ford would be for me and Mom to drive while Dad was at work. The problem with the Ford was that I kept stripping a gear in the transmission. I could drop the transmission and replace the cluster gear in two hours. Dad was convinced that I was the problem and not the transmission or the Ford. He completely rebuilt the transmission himself and only Mom drove the car for two weeks. The transmission went out again. Dad repaired it once more and then traded it for my dream car, a 1949 Oldsmobile Fastback.

Automobiles – 1949 Oldsmobile Fastback

There were more strings attached to the purchase of the 1949 Oldsmobile. This would be my car and I would need to have a loan from the bank. At fifteen, I had my first official debt. I received a loan from the Aransas Pass Bank (cosigned by Dad) for enough to pay insurance for one year, purchase the car and purchase the parts for a complete engine overhaul. The loan payment would be $50 a month. Another job was in my future. The lecture at the bank included establishing good credit and the perils of a bad credit rating. I could destroy the entire family's credit since Dad was my cosigner. I shared this important lesson with my children before they got to drive.

I had enough on my plate with school, football, and hopefully girls and a new job. I took the advice to heart and out of fear, (sort of like a mortal sin) I managed to avoid the hell of bad credit.

Dick, Jerrie and 1949 Black Oldsmobile - 2019

Once the car loan was secured, I was in debt for a car that was almost as cool as my friend Rodney's Ford. Dad took the car to his friend's auto repair garage in Beeville, and we completely rebuilt the engine on weekends. This was a special time with Dad. Spending time together and overhauling an automobile engine was as good as having Dad as my football coach in junior high school. Football and autos were two areas where Dad had a magic touch.

Later, in typical teenage fashion, I took that *like-new engine* out and replaced it with a larger engine that wasn't like new. Another lesson learned the hard way.

The joy of that 1949 Oldsmobile with its glass pack mufflers was a happy time for me. An American V-8 engine was music to my ears. I remember overhearing Dad telling Mom there are much worse habits Dick could get hooked on than constantly tinkering with cars and being excited about machinery.

I am glad I was raised in Ingleside where being a rebel was racking your mufflers at an inappropriate time and being willing to apologize.

AMERICAN MACHINERY AND SUBMARINES

Machinery continued to amaze me after high school. I fell in love with the General Motors 16-cylinder diesel engines that powered our country's submarines from World War II.

During my first hitch in the Navy, I had the privilege of going to sleep to the rumble of those big diesel engines on my first submarine, the USS Capitaine (SS-336). I qualified as an Engine Room Oiler before I qualified in my rating of Sonar. I knew engines, but I was just learning Sonar.

I moved on to nuclear submarines where absolute quiet was the goal. I still loved to listen to those last diesel submarines as they charged their batteries.

Most Americans probably do not know that the USS Cavalla (SS-244) sits in Galveston, Texas at Seawolf Park. The USS Cavalla is the WWII Diesel Submarine that sunk the Japanese Aircraft Carrier that launched the attack on Pearl Harbor. When you tour the USS Cavalla, you will be proud of America and her craftsmen. In every detail, she looks ready to go to sea. Jerrie, who is not easily impressed, was in awe as we toured the USS Cavalla. I was able to explain in detail the purpose of machines, pumps, and valves on the boat. Yes, we call a submarine a boat. I showed her where my first bunk, that was not a hot bunk or torpedo skid bunk, was located. I qualified on a similar submarine more than sixty years ago.

If the USS Cavalla engines were still functional, I'm sure I could fire up one of those big diesel engines. I loved those submarines.

My love affair with submarines soon focused on Nuclear Powered Fast Attack Submarines that helped end the Cold War. The second-generation USS Cavalla (SSN-684) was my favorite class of Fast Attack Submarines. American submarines and warships are superior to any in the world. American shipbuilders are still superior craftsmen in a world that often no longer values craftsmanship.

| USS Cavalla (SS-244)

| USS Cavalla (SSN-684)

My 1949 Oldsmobile was the beginning of my love affair with American built machinery. In the 1940s and 1950s, American automobiles were superior machines. My 1949 Oldsmobile was my only car during my high school years. The Oldsmobile was passed on, in Ingleside, after my time. Many years later, one of the future owners was still complaining about that "damned engine you put in the first Rocket 88." I also passed on my 1953 Oldsmobile convertible in Ingleside a few years later. I have not heard any complaints about the convertible.

After my nuclear submarine days, I prefer ultra-quiet to the sound of glass-packs.

THE PAPER ROUTE

To support my dream car and my social life I took over a large paper route that covered Ingleside, Old Ingleside, and the surrounding countryside to the city limits of Aransas Pass. I delivered the Corpus Christi Caller-Times every day. This paper route took most of my time outside of school. Every morning at 4:00 am, I was up rolling newspapers, sometimes with the help of family and friends. Dad was already an expert at rolling papers; just another of his amazing and diverse talents. Mom was a quick learner and I think she enjoyed driving the route on occasion.

If I wanted to get paid, I had to learn to manage money. I received a bill from the Caller-Times. To pay that bill, I had to collect from every customer. My pay was whatever was left after I paid the Caller-Times.

Dad helped me to set up my accounts and helped me develop a process for collecting and accounting for money. I also got help from Mr. Kanis, the business teacher at Ingleside High School. I felt like a businessman.

Dealing with customers was a big part of the job. I had never heard of the word introvert, but I knew that talking to folks was not easy for me. Mom took most of the calls for a missed paper and I seldom missed a paper so that was not a big problem.

Collecting was my problem. Like my Grandad PW, I did best with the ladies. I decided that girls were trained to be nice. I had a couple of men on the route that would always make me come back several times to get paid and one that always paid me with a one-hundred-dollar bill. I still remember his name, but I will not share it. The ladies that I remember knew when I was coming and often had cookies and cold milk for me. No wonder PW preferred dealing with the ladies.

The paper route was a big job considering my other school obligations, but I could not give it up. I loved driving the route and I liked the financial independence it provided. I tried cotton picking for three days before I threw in the sack. I did not have the skill, or the stamina, to be a cotton picker. I would much rather get up at 4:00 a.m. and drive my car on a paper route. I was average at just about everything else, but I was a great paperboy.

My football coach, Emory Bellard, said that I was a great paperboy. He never said that about my football skills. I could throw Coach Bellard's paper out the passenger window while driving by at 25 mph and put his paper exactly where he wanted it. If he were outside waiting for his paper, as he often was, I would rack my mufflers just to say, "Good morning, Coach." I knew he was right about my skills, but I also knew there were no scholarships for accuracy in throwing newspapers.

Moving into the Garage

Granny Morrow, from Beeville, came to live with us in Ingleside after Grandad (PW) passed. I am not sure why she lost her home, but I know that it was a traumatic event. With PW gone, the Grand Old House was the center of her life.

Our small house became overcrowded. We had two bedrooms and one bath to hold a high school student, an elementary school student, Mom, Dad, and Granny. Granny took the bedroom my brother and I normally shared. My brother, Charles alternated between Mom and Dad's bedroom and the couch. Dad built me a sleeping loft in the eaves of our single car garage. There was just enough room for a mattress. It worked great and was good preparation for my life on a submarine. It was hot, but everyone was hot. No one that I knew in Ingleside had air conditioning. I put a fan in the eaves to control the heat.

I could have a couple of pinups if they were not too unclad. The pinups had to be out of sight when Mom changed the sheets and did her inspections on Mondays. Pinups were not very revealing in the 1950s. I was the only kid to have a legal pinup in his room even if that room was just a mattress in the garage.

My loft was like camping out all the time and it was convenient for the paper route. We had no close neighbors on the garage side of the house except the Patio Bar. The diehards were gone from The Patio by the time I started rolling papers.

INGLESIDE HIGH SCHOOL

When I began school in Ingleside for the second semester of eighth grade, there were students in my class that had been my classmates in first grade, when I lived in Ingleside the first time. I did not recognize any of them.

St. Joseph's Catholic School in Beeville had prepared me for the academic work at Ingleside. Academics were not my problem. I made good grades in the new school, which pleased Mom. I could not talk to Mom about the differences that I noticed between St. Joseph's and Ingleside's schools. In addition to Ingleside being a public school with no church across the street for my quiet time, they had seventh and eighth grade combined with high school, which meant that I was going to school with full-grown men and women.

It was commonplace for Jimmy, the tight end on the football team, to peel out in front of the school in a cool Oldsmobile and no one paid any attention. Sister Agnes would have had a heart attack. I noticed that some of the grown women were quite attractive. I wondered if any of them would talk to me. I also wondered if I could play football with these grown men. All my old fears related to school were in high gear. I finally worked up the courage to dump my school fears on Dad. I told Dad that all I can think about is pretty girls, fast cars, and football. What should I do? He gave me one of his simple answers.

"It's just hormones, don't worry about it."

I could not do anything about the pretty girls or fast cars, so I decided to focus on football.

First Educator / Coaching Role Model – Coach Haugen

While I was still in eighth grade, and after listening to stories about Coach Haugen, the Assistant Football Coach, I found myself slipping out of study hall to listen to him in his History class. There was no football discussed in Coach Haugen's class. He always seemed to be telling a story of some great consequence and the students in the class were sitting quietly. This was unlike my other classes. I knew that I would need to enroll in history next year. I wanted to get to know Coach Haugen well.

By the time I got to Coach Haugen's history class, I had already met him in the fall football practices. During football practice, I decided that I liked this quiet gentleman who helped us endure over 100-degree temperature and 100 percent humidity and whatever new torture Coach Bellard had in mind. Coach Haugen encouraged us when we felt we could give no more. From the older football players, I learned that Coach Haugen was a military veteran and was very patriotic. I was also told that he would encourage us to prepare for college. No one in my family had gone to college but the idea intrigued me.

Coach Haugen was the Head Basketball Coach. He was an assistant coach in several other sports and drove the school bus. Mr. Haugen and Coach Haugen were the only two names that he would respond to from students. He believed that we needed to learn that rules were a part of life. Coach Haugen downplayed his military service. He suggested *it's just what Americans do when they're needed.* This sounded like what my Uncle Billy and my Uncle Gene might say. They were all heroes to me.

Coach Haugen was an advocate for higher education for every student that could benefit from college. He was unlike any other teacher I experienced in high school. He was what I imagined a college professor would be. He always told his students, at the beginning of the class, that we were responsible for every word in the textbook and that he would be talking about the same topics as the textbook but what he told us would likely not be in the textbook. For every period of every class, he would tell us history stories and you could hear a pin drop as he walked around talking without notes about the most serious issues on the planet. Those of us who played sports for him knew that there had been lots of preparation before class. To have a class of high school students listen quietly and attentively was unusual. None of us wanted to disappoint Coach Haugen.

I did not run into a history professor who taught like Coach Haugen until years later when, as a college professor, I would slip into the back of the Civil War History class being taught by my friend and colleague Dr. Terry Jones as he would tell stories of the Civil War.

Mr. Haugen was a man of calm demeanor and was a true gentleman. This persona followed him outside the classroom and even to the football field.

On occasion, when Coach Haugen was in the basketball arena, he could be a different person. Games always began with a gentleman coach. As the game progressed a more intense coach emerged. Coach did not get out of hand and never directed his angst against a player. I remember a time when I saw him grab the back of a folding chair with a death grip. I thought *No, Coach! Don't throw the chair!*

The referees were almost in shock that this wonderful coach could be so upset. The fans were silent. Then, Coach threw up his hands, walked to the other end of the player's bench, and sat down. The gym went crazy. Had this gentleman coach stared the other coach and the referees down?

I'm not sure of the dynamics at play but we won the game and the coach never spoke another word until the game was over. Meanwhile, a quiet young player from Ingleside, named Attaway, took over on the court and dominated the rest of the game. At the end of the game, Coach shook hands with everyone, and we went home. I often wondered if this show of intensity was part of a hidden plan or a spontaneous reaction. Other coaches were intense all the time, but not Coach Haugen.

In my professional life, I tried to emulate Coach Haugen. I do recall a few occasions when a more intense persona emerged. These instances shocked people because it was out of character. I noticed that the young men involved never bent the rules again. I occasionally receive phone calls from some of these young men who are now senior citizens. They might say, "Master Chief, is that you? How are you doing? Are you okay? You saved me from myself when I was young and dumb. Please call me if you ever need any help." Although the more intense behavior was effective, it was certainly unplanned and not a behavior I would plan to repeat. I suspect the same was true of Coach Haugen.

After Ingleside, I believe Coach Haugen returned to Texas Lutheran College, his Alma Mater, and worked there until he retired. I know that was where his heart was, but I am thankful for the ten years that Ingleside was able to have a person of his character to influence the lives of kids like me. I admire the work of Coach Haugen, even his basketball intensity. He was a real person.

My wife and I attended his funeral at the First Lutheran Church in Seguin, Texas when he passed at age 87. The obituary for Robert Bob Harrison Haugen described the quiet man that he was. I was amazed that, in his obituary, his military service and his body of work with young men and women at Ingleside High School for ten years was summed up in a short statement. Probably just the way he would have wanted it. Coach Haugen was a valued mentor and is a role model for my life.

Coach Bellard and Billy Fred

During the second semester of eighth grade, I had Health Class with the Head Football Coach for the Ingleside football team, Coach Emory Bellard. Coach Bellard taught me more about football than he did about health, but that was all right with me. Earning my letter in football was my primary goal. Football would solve my fears as a new kid in town. I knew I could learn health from the textbook.

By the end of that semester, I knew the names of the returning football players and their positions. I decided that I would try out for fullback. My reasoning was simple. The current fullback, Billy Fred, seemed to have befriended me and was willing to help me get ready for *two a day* practices in the fall. I needed all the help I could get to be a letterman in my freshman year, like Dad.

That goal to be a **Freshman Letterman** became my single focus, and girls and cars faded on my priority list. Billy Fred was a junior in high school so he would be my senior next year when I was a freshman.

When Coach Bellard heard my plan to be a fullback, he said, "We'll see, we don't even know if you can run into people, get up and run into them again without hurting yourself."

I'm not sure I ever impressed Coach Bellard with my football skills, but he impressed me with his coaching skills. He looked at all the kids he had available for the football team and saw the basic pieces he had to work with as pieces of a jigsaw puzzle. Coach viewed each player individually.

His question about me was, "Will all this enthusiasm for the game be combined with a love for contact? **Will he love to hit, will he love to block and tackle?**"

Coach had been telling me all along what he needed to know but I had not been listening. **"Can you run into people, get up and run into them again and not hurt yourself?"**

When Coach found out in spring drills that I loved to hit, and that I usually did not hurt myself, he made a very small place for me, as he put the puzzle together for the 1953-1954 Ingleside Mustangs.

Coach put the pieces of the puzzle together and a football

powerhouse emerged.

After Ingleside, Coach Bellard performed his magic at many high schools and colleges.

When Emory Bellard developed the Wishbone Offense that took the University of Texas to the National Championship, he was just working the Emory Bellard magic. He analyzed the talent available on the team and put them together in an offense that took advantage of a unique and talented skill set. Defensive Coordinators were not prepared for the Wishbone Offense with players who seemed to be born to play their assigned position.

I'm glad I had two years to watch a genius at work. I'm also glad that he found a place for a kid who had only two things going for him, the love of the game and the love to hit. Football is a contact sport.

Billy Fred was a great mentor for me. More than half a century later, we sat together at Coach Bellard's induction into the Texas Sports Hall of Fame. In typical Ingleside fashion, we visited and joked as if we had seen each other yesterday, rather than the fact we had not seen each other in many years. Billy Fred also shared with me the reason he adopted me. Coach Bellard had asked him to get me off his back. He told Billy Fred, "He's driving me crazy with all of his questions."

I said, "I thought you picked me as your freshman because you thought I would be a good fullback."

Billy Fred responded, "There you go, thinking again."

FOOTBALL POWERHOUSE

During my freshman and sophomore year, Ingleside High School was a small school football powerhouse. At that time, schools our size could only advance as far as regional competition. Ingleside won the southern region of Texas decisively. We were undefeated and untied for two seasons, a total of twenty-four games. Many football analysts suggested that Ingleside was one of the best teams in Texas of any size. I am not sure that was true, however, we had an amazing football team. We had a small group of athletes that had exceptional talent. We had an extremely talented head football coach. Many people feel that Emory Bellard was one of the best high school and college football coaches in the history of Texas Football. We also had an assistant coach that was an exceptional team builder, Coach Robert Haugen. The rest of the team, of which I was a part, was enthusiastic, hardworking, and often played well above our talent level. We had a community of parents and supporters for whom our team was a matter of great pride. Ingleside football games were worth shutting down much of the business community on Friday nights.

Any team today that had a core of talent, like the players from the two undefeated seasons, could win a football title in any era. In my freshman year, the first of the two undefeated seasons, I worked hard as the back-up fullback for Billy Fred. As a freshman, I earned my first football letter. Goal accomplished. I also learned that year that my love of the game, and my love for hitting, would need to compensate for a lack of natural talent. I was not fast. I could not make the moves of Billy Fred's little brother, John, but I did love to hit.

After earning my letter as a backup fullback during my freshman year, Coach Bellard switched me to the line, linebacker, and special teams in my sophomore year. My mentor, Billy Fred, graduated after my freshman year.

MACK – MY NEW MENTOR

I picked a new player to be my unofficial, and possibly unknown to him, football mentor. Mack was special because he not only was a great football player, but he was smart and willing to let me pick his brain. Mack went on to play football for Rice Institute. Mack was on the Rice football team when they won the Southwest Conference Championship. Mack had the opportunity to play in major bowl games while at Rice. I quietly cheered for Rice and Mack from faraway places.

When I converted from fullback for my sophomore year, I was what today is called a special team's player. Mack taught me to focus when I was on the field to defend kick returns, punt returns, and to block punts.

For a player without a great deal of natural talent, I became good in this position and made many tackles and blocked several punts. I still use the focus skills I developed as a special team's player to ignore distractions when I need to concentrate on important tasks.

The quality of my special team's play earned me playing time as a linebacker, offensive guard, and defensive tackle. I was pretty beefed up and I earned the nickname Bear which I had forgotten about till I saw folks wishing The Bear well when I pulled out an old yearbook.

While I was not a starter in my sophomore year, I played a high percentage of each game at one position or another. I enjoyed the game of football more in my sophomore year than at any time before or after.

There was a downside to the type of player that I became in my sophomore year. In practice, I was always on the defense against the starting offense. The reason the team did not need me at fullback was that our new offense did not use a full-time fullback and when they did need a fullback, they had Lee. In four years of football, I was never hit as hard by any player as when I attempted to stop Lee at the line of scrimmage. Each time, even when successful, I would ask myself if rattling my brain was worth the effort. I kept going back for more.

I did earn my letter in my sophomore year of football. I loved every minute of my sophomore year, as an Ingleside Mustang football player. I was certain I made at least a small contribution to the undefeated season.

***

THE LOSING SEASON

My junior year in high school was a good year in many ways, but that did not include the record of the football team. We lost every game.

In our defense, we lost all but four starters from the regional championship team. Coach Bellard left to take larger schools to state championships. We had no head coach until just before school started and we moved to a conference of larger schools. The conference was due to the periodic conference realignment. Many Ingleside folks thought that the realignment was simply to stop Ingleside's football dominance. It accomplished that goal but not for long. Ingleside won a state championship several years later. That future was no help for the 1955 - 1956 Mustangs.

It was hard to find a talented head football coach when you had only four returning starters and were moving to a larger conference. The pay for coaches at Ingleside was peanuts and coaches were responsible for many tasks outside of football.

We lost all 10 games and the new coach resigned.

The losing season was not the fault of the new coach. Coach lost the team's support early in the season when he walked out at halftime in frustration and did not return for the rest of that game. We held together as a team with the help of Coach Haugen. We were competitive during several games and we came close to winning on a couple of occasions. I have a nightmare about one of the close games. I blocked a punt, and the ball went into the end zone where I kicked the ball out of the end zone trying to cover it for a touchdown. The facts of the play were true. I am not sure it happened in a game we could have won.

I learned about the bond of teammates that year. Somewhere during the losing season, we returned to playing football for the love of the game and the opportunity to play football together as we represented our school. After losing the first game by 28-0 and falling behind in the first half of the George West game which we eventually lost 33-7, I did not play my best. I was not a great player, but I was a team leader. I was not playing like a team leader.

When I got home from the game, Dad said "I was ashamed of your effort tonight and I will bet that you're ashamed also. Give it your best every game or quit."

That was the low point for me. I did not quit, and the team got my best for the rest of the season. Few of us considered leaving the team. Most of our classmates supported us. Coach Haugen supported us in what he referred to as a difficult situation.

The community was not that supportive. They lived to win. Dad was one of the most supportive of the fans. He understood the problem of playing larger schools. He had been the volunteer head coach at St. Joseph's School when I was in seventh and eighth grade. We always played much larger schools. Under Dad, I learned about moral victories, team building, and the joy of playing football as a game. Somewhere along the path to defeat on the scoreboard, the 1955- 1956 Mustangs rediscovered the fun of playing football. Most of us became lifelong teammates.

RW

In one of our losing home games where we made a good showing, RW was our secret weapon. He had been injured the week before and was grounded for the current game. He reverted to his favorite activity when he was not on the football field. He drove the new coach crazy with his incessant talking, good humor, and suggestions. Even the patient Coach Haugen began to be distracted by RW. Coach Haugen came up with one of his greatest tactical coaching suggestions.

"Let's send RW to be the spotter for the announcer in the booth, on the top row of the stadium."

Well, as was his way, RW took over the announcer's booth, and his good humor lifted the gloom and doom atmosphere that prevailed on the Ingleside bench.

Keith Nix and I were the first to notice what RW was doing to spark his teammates. From the announcer's booth came RW's voice.

"That last play was a spectacular example of great defense and teamwork. Nix hit the runner low and Witte came in with the final crushing blow, about chest high."

All the action on the play had been in the middle of the line, where it was impossible to see what happened. Except Keith and I knew we were only marginally involved. We speculated that RW had made a mistake. Then, it became clear that RW had made a script that ran just behind the action. Without modern instant replay, it was difficult to dispute what he was saying.

Nix and Witte dominated on defense in the first half, making tackles all over the field, and sometimes when one of us was on the bench. During the second half, he had Dean, Richardson, and Davis join Witte and Nix to dominate on defense. It was amazing that the opposing team managed to score, with this strong defense.

RW also helped to get the few fans who still came to the Mustang games involved in the action. He stirred up the fans against the referees to the point that we all started to believe him.

From the announcer's booth, RW shouted, "Can you believe that call? That was a perfect pass from Stewart into the end zone. The receiver only dropped the pass because of interference. The referee is refusing to call interference. Ingleside should be up by one touchdown, rather than down by one touchdown."

It took a huddle with the referees and the coaches to get RW grounded. By that time, the fans were incensed! RW began hobbling up and down the sidelines and continued to stir things up. We still lost, but it was a close game and we had a great time. RW, our teammate, had made football a game again. The fact that we almost won was just icing on the cake.

RW was probably right about Keith being involved in almost every defensive play. Keith was one of the toughest guys I would ever know.

For years, I would get phone calls from RW, with a disguised voice, like a character out of some great plot. One year, it was the voice from the IRS, with details of an impending audit. A few years later, there was a call about delinquent speeding tickets. According to the call, the Highway Patrol had begun issuing radar speeding tickets, and I had amassed a pile of tickets and could go to jail. In our current era of telephone scams, RW could have made a fortune. But RW was not in it for the money. He was in it for the fun.

FOOTBALL - SENIOR YEAR

In my senior year, we were again a competitive football team. We had a new head coach, Coach Wagner. We also had Coach Haugen and

Coach Holloman. Several players from this team received district honors and scholarship offers.

The importance of football in small-town Texas cannot be overemphasized. In the 1955 -1956 Yearbook - The Mustang, three full pages were devoted to coverage of the losing football team. The track team, tennis team, and volleyball team shared a single page. In the 1956 -1957 yearbook, we made progress in sharing with the other sports. The Mustang had a full page devoted to Robin Cox and Jerry Lou Wright going to State in tennis.

ACADEMIC ISSUES AND GREAT TEACHERS

In addition to a losing football season, I found that I was having difficulty with some of my academic work. Part of the problem was too much on my plate with the distractions of cars, sports, paper route, and trying to impress the opposite sex. I was not a great student, but it was a real eye-opener for me when I realized that, without help, I was probably going to fail one and possibly two classes. The two classes were chemistry and typing.

Chemistry and typing were different classes. Chemistry challenged my intellect and typing was like piano lessons all over again. I was a piano dropout, but I couldn't afford to be a typing dropout. My lack of natural talent and my lack of patience to stick with tasks that were hard for me contributed to my predicament.

CHEMISTRY

For chemistry, I threw myself on the mercy of my teacher. My chemistry teacher was also the Superintendent of Schools for the Ingleside School System, Mr. OT Blaschke. He had been my geometry teacher and while the class was difficult, I never considered that I might fail. Mr. Blaschke knew I was usually a good student. I convinced him that I was still a good student but was having difficulty with chemistry. I won him over. He did not give me any slack in class, but he did agree to tutor me outside of class. I got key chemistry instruction two times.

I doubt there is any place other than Ingleside Texas where the school superintendent would take the time to tutor an average student in chemistry on his own time and without charge. Mr. Blaschke was not your average school superintendent. He was a teacher first and academics and student success were most important to him.

I passed chemistry but decided that I was not quite as smart as I thought. I decided I wasn't smart enough to be an engineer and inventor like Grandpa Witte. The scales began to tip away from college and toward joining the U.S. Navy.

Perhaps I should have trusted Mr. Blaschke. He told me that I was smart enough to be anything I wanted to be if I was willing to work hard and challenge myself. He said I had worked hard and was successful in a difficult science class. He recommended I should go ahead and take physics.

I declined that advice only to find that when I got to college, I loved physics and made straight A's. Learning to trust your great teachers is an important part of education.

TYPING

The typing class was a different challenge. Just trying hard and studying would not help. Typing had so much in common with my failure at piano lessons. Typing was a skill that I could not master. There was no school superintendent in the typing class. My teacher said that typing was like a game of sports, you either got to the finish line or you didn't. Do the work and do it well enough to pass the time and accuracy requirements.

In typical Ingleside fashion, the equivalent of teammates came to my rescue. Several girls from my class became my coaches. They did not do my work, but they treated it like practice in a sport, they had me do the equivalent of wind sprints in typing. They had me do the typing exercises over and over until I managed to complete the work in the time required and without excessive mistakes. Thanks to my typing teammates, I passed Typing I. They gave me a hand, but not a handout. I did well enough that it was even suggested that I go ahead and take Typing II. I appreciated my typing teammates, but I declined.

Now, all these years later, I develop this memory with a #2 pencil before I move to the computer's word processing software. Some lessons I just needed to learn the hard way.

BAND

I tried music one more time by signing up for band class. In truth, I just wanted to be around my band friends. Mr. Hipp, Ingleside's Band Director, seemed to understand my motivation.

He said, "Let's start you on the drum pad and see how it goes."

I never got off the drum pad. I dropped band class as an academic subject. I did have several academic success stories besides passing chemistry and typing.

NUMBER SENSE

The first of these successes came from listening to good advice from a great teacher. Mrs. Florence Haugen was an exceptional math and science teacher. Mrs. Haugen taught me Algebra I and Algebra II and told me that I would get a lot out of an elective course she was going to teach called Number Sense. I took the class, and I have used the practical skills learned in that class every day of my life. Thank you, Florence Haugen.

Homemaking

I signed up for another interesting elective called Homemaking. The class was taught by Fay Taylor. I thought *this will be a great way to meet and be around girls.* What I remember most about this class was how much I loved the class and not just because there were girls in the class. I learned valuable skills. I use these skills every day. I was marginal in sewing, but I learned enough to serve me in an emergency. I loved cooking and the kitchen tools of the trade. I even loved the kitchen clean-up.

Fay Taylor was a great teacher with a wonderful sense of humor. She not only told us about cooking and baking but she showed us how to do it and how much fun we could have. No wonder Granny loved her kitchen. Fay let us know that cooking was not just for girls. I had no TV to watch great male chefs. In my family, men cooked on the river bottom or the beach in a sandpit but never in the kitchen. I told Earl Swinney, my future father-in-law, how much fun the homemaking class had been. He said to wait until you taste my German Chocolate Cake. Earl was a great cook and was forever surprising me.

Earl told me a great cooking story about the crews who worked to keep the pipeline tank farms and remote stations maintained. The work crews were called pipeline gangs and they camped and cooked their meals on-site much like the old cattle drives. Each gang had a cook who provided basic but healthy food for men who worked hard. Earl had worked with the gangs and loved to visit with the guys when they worked the tank farms near Ingleside. He decided to bake them one of his German Chocolate Cakes in a heavy sheet cake pan. He took the cake to the campsite and left it with the cook. All the workers were still working off-site when he visited.

About a week later he saw one of the workers and said, "I heard you guys had German Chocolate Cake last week."

The worker said, "Jose is such a great cook. He baked that cake on the campfire! He told us it was his secret cake."

Earl went back to get his cake pan from Jose and asked, "How did they like the cake?"

Jose said, "They liked it. They thought I cooked it. I told them it was my secret cake. What a joke."

Earl gave Jose his little smile and took his pan. Earl was a man who seldom talked but baked a good story and a great cake.

My kitchen skills turned out to be important in my first year on a submarine. Each new crew member on a submarine was required to spend at least one month working as a mess cook. How well we performed this duty made a lasting impression on our shipmates. Mealtime was the only leisure time on a submarine. Thanks to Fay Taylor, I was a good mess cook and that gave me a head start on being a great submariner. The galley on a submarine was small but even the oldest submarine had modern kitchen tools. The senior cook on a submarine often had advanced culinary training and was considered by most Commanding Officers to be the best Morale Officer he could have. The cooks could tell I liked working with them.

I still use my kitchen skills every day. I am not a chef, but I'm a good short-order cook. I have developed considerable expertise in using kitchen tools to create healthy fruit and vegetable dishes. For at least the last fifteen years, I have been creating ultra-healthy vegetable and fruit smoothies. These smoothies are probably why the former Bear is still around. Thank you, Fay.

VIVIAN SHELDON

Another special teacher at Ingleside High School was Vivian Sheldon. Mrs. Sheldon convinced us that we were capable writers even when we did marginal work. I am sure I never met Vivian's expectations, but I still believed I could write. Such a nice person would not tell me I was capable if I was not. With that belief, I have attempted several difficult projects and at least a few would have received a passing grade in Vivian's class. Perhaps I will still do something that Vivian would give an A-. Stranger things have happened.

LEON TAYLOR

Leon Taylor was an extraordinary educator who put students before the letter of the law. I still have not figured out how he knew that RW and I planned an escape from Study Hall for a day at the beach in the spring of 1957. We did not tell a soul and yet when we jumped out of the Study Hall window, he was there to say, "Got You!" That was the beginning of a different afternoon than we had planned.

OT BLASCHKE

I often thought over the years that the greatest accomplishment of OT Blaschke was helping me pass high school chemistry. I know that he very quietly did many things for the students of Ingleside High School. One of the most important of those accomplishments was ensuring that our students had exceptional teachers like the ones I have just described.

SOCIAL LIFE

My social life, outside of sports in the 1950s, revolved around the youth centers in Ingleside and Aransas Pass, the homes of some pretty progressive parents, activities sponsored by the school system, and special places in Ingleside and Aransas Pass that welcomed teenagers.

YOUTH CENTERS

From the time I went with my parents to the dance halls in Cuero, I imagined that I could become a dancer. In Ingleside and Aransas Pass, our dance halls were the youth centers. After we settled in Ingleside, I shared my vision with Mom. First, she tried to be my dance instructor. That was more of a challenge than she could manage, so she set out to get some help. She signed me up for ballroom dancing. While I'm sure that I was a challenge to the ballroom dance instructor, I gained enough confidence in dancing that I enjoyed every minute at the youth centers. I accepted that I would never be able to compete with talented dancers like my friend Jeffrey, who was a natural dancer and a great athlete. With practice, I developed a level of comfort and enjoyment in dancing that I still enjoy today. Jerrie and I dance at least one song every day whenever the spirit moves us. We dance barefoot, on the carpet, or the kitchen floor. On occasion, we go to Sun City Texas dances. They are like youth center dances for old people. There are always several talented dancers, but we hold our own in the slow dances.

Occasionally, someone will ask, "How long have you been dancing together?"

We usually answer; "Only a little over sixty years, but we plan to take some lessons."

HOME OF FRIENDS

Many of my friends had progressive parents. These folks seemed to understand that if you wanted to know where your children were, make them feel welcome in your home. The guy houses were primarily where we met as guys and talked cars and other things that in the 1950s we considered guy topics. When there was a gathering of guys and girls, it was usually at a girl's house. That was just the way it was.

GUY HOUSES

I had many friends whose parents welcomed me into their homes. These guy houses were each a little different but were homes where my guy friends were always welcome.

THE WITTE HOUSE

Friends who felt welcome in our home usually were the guys who knew that they could get something to eat from Mom and knew that Dad was a soft touch to help them with their cars. We did not have a home that was big enough for parties, but our garage had every tool that you could need to work on a car. You could also park your car and even leave it overnight if there was a big repair needed. Our hot rods and drag races were important to us, and they were mostly conducted with parental approval and sometimes with their participation. It was not unusual that the town Constable would keep traffic clear until a drag race was finished.

Unwritten rules kept most of us safe most of the time. Dad was known for both his expertise with cars and his honest opinion. Even when we did not want to hear his opinion, if you worked on your car at the Witte house you were going to get the opinion of Herbert Witte. If Dad said, "That will never work" you knew it would not work. If Dad said, "That should work" you could be sure that your project was at least safe.

I thank the good Lord for keeping me and most of my friends safe from ourselves and our teenage impulses. I'm also glad that Dad helped two generations of teenagers keep their cars running and safe.

RODNEY'S HOUSE

Another great guy house was Rodney's House. Rodney had the coolest car of any of my friends. His 1950 Ford Coupe was nice to look at and had a great sound. Rodney's mom was a great cook. She never seemed to mind giving us a taste. Thanks to my friendship with Rodney, I also had another great experience that involved American trucks and machinery. Rodney's family allowed me to join Rodney in driving a grain truck one season. I still remember that 1954 GMC Grain Truck like it was yesterday. I thought it was beautiful.

I still think that the 1949 -1954 GMC and Chevy trucks are some of the most beautiful trucks ever built. It was not the farm work I enjoyed, but the company of Rodney and getting the chance to drive a great truck. If I live long enough, perhaps I will buy a 1954 GMC or Chevy five-window pickup. On second thought, I think I will just be happy with my current Chevy pickup named Silver, after the Lone Ranger's beloved steed.

I need to get in touch with Rodney and meet for lunch, even if we both need to drive a couple of hours to meet. We could tell a few stories from the days when we hauled grain and drove hot rods.

When I told an acquaintance about this unexecuted plan, she said, "That's a long drive to tell a few stories."

After a little reflection, I've decided there are few things more important than old friends meeting and telling stories. I am going to make it a priority, this year, to meet more old friends and tell stories.

RW's House and Drive-In Store

While we did not work on cars at RW's, both his family's Drive-In store and their home was a place we were always welcome. There was lots of food in both places. Beginning in my sophomore year, I seemed to have had an endless appetite. I guess that's how I earned the nickname Bear. I must have been like one of those bears in our national parks, always looking for another meal.

RW and I had a good scam going for a while. We figured out how we could both eat two suppers every night. Since our families ate supper at different times, we came up with a storyline, concocted by RW, as to why I was eating at his house and he was eating at our house every night. This ploy worked wonderfully for several weeks until our moms happened to meet at Tommy's IGA. They had suspected we were working a scam but didn't care. They would have continued to feed us supper at both houses every night, but we decided it would be gossip too soon. We went back to grabbing an extra supper when there was something special on the menu.

GIRL HOUSES

The girl houses were a group of homes in Ingleside, near the high school, where several young ladies lived. Some were my friends, and some were prospects for the more serious category of girlfriend. I was lucky that the girls I called friends had parents who seemed to welcome me into their homes. It was nice to have a group of homes where you were welcomed by the parents as well as their teenage daughters. One of these girls, Jerrie, has lived with me for over 60 years. Several of these girls still live in Ingleside. All these girls are lifetime friends. I need to check in with my Ingleside friends.

One of my Ingleside friends who was a girl emerged as my girlfriend. Then, she emerged as my soul mate. During my last two years at Ingleside High School, Jerrie Swinney and I did almost everything together. The Swinney House is my example of a girl house. Jerrie's friends and mine were always welcome. Jerrie and I are still doing things together. Perhaps the secret of an enduring relationship is to be great friends with the entire family.

THE SWINNEY HOUSE

Jerrie's Dad, Earl Swinney, was a significant role model for me. Earl was the only person I knew, other than some of the coaches, who played college football. After playing football at South Park High School in Beaumont, Texas, Earl went on to play at Lamar Tech, now Lamar University.

Earl had the coolest 1955 Ford Two Door Hard Top in town. When I threw the Swinney newspaper, I was extremely careful to keep the paper away from the Ford. My family was a General Motors family, so Earl's 1955 Ford joined Rodney's 1950 Ford Two Door Sedan and the 1940 Ford Coupe that Dad restored as the only Fords I have ever coveted.

Earl, like Dad, was a great fisherman. He fished almost every day, either before or after work. Earl had the luxury of fishing from the Sun Oil Company's docks, where he was employed as an engineer on the pipeline. Earl was sort of like Grandpa Witte and Granny Morrow. He was not much of a talker, but he was a great listener. I was comfortable talking to Earl because he was the ultimate guy. He understood guy concerns, even though he was living in a house of girls. The only other guy in the house was his dog Pug. Since Earl was more a listener than a talker, a big response was either a smile or a chuckle. A real challenging response was a disapproving look or when he called me *Fat Boy* to let me know what he thought about my beefing up for football plan.

| Earl Swinney

I met Jerrie's little sister, Judy, for the first time when she was about nine years old. I went to their home to pick up Jerrie for a date. As I walked under a tree, at the edge of the street, I heard a voice from above. "Excuse me, excuse me." When I realized that I was being spoken to from the tree, I looked up and a voice said, "You are going to need to help me down from this tree. I got up here without any trouble, but I can't figure out how to get down."

I was directed to the garage, where I retrieved a ladder and we completed the rescue. With feet on the ground, Judy said, "Thank you. Who are you and what are you doing at my house?"

I could tell from the little smile that she knew exactly who I was, so I said, "My name is Dick and I came to rescue you."

Jerrie's Mom, Bea Swinney, was a great cook, and because Earl kept the family with a supply of fresh fish, the Swinney family had fresh fish and homemade lemon pie at least once each week. Judy, who graduated later from Ingleside High School, was quoted as saying, "Oh no, not fish and lemon pie again!" Bea would just shake her head and keep cooking.

I was popular with Bea because I loved her cooking and she said that I was not afraid of washing dishes. I was as comfortable at the Swinney home as I was the Witte home. I was glad that Jerrie turned out to be a great girlfriend.

JERRIE SWINNEY

Jerrie Swinney was to band what I wanted to be in football. She was a natural talent. In the Concert Band, she played the oboe and sometimes the flute and the saxophone. Earlier in her childhood, she had even played the violin. In the Marching Band, she was a Drum Majorette. I thought she was the most beautiful girl I had ever seen.

While I could not watch the half-time performances of the Ingleside Marching Band at football games, I attended every concert that the band played during my junior and senior years at Ingleside High School. I appreciated my band friends and wanted to be around them by going to their concerts, even if I could not master an instrument. I would bet that Bobby Sterns is still playing his horn.

Jerrie was an excellent academic student and she would later become an outstanding middle school teacher. She earned the nickname *The Terminator* when she took a group of kids from a small country school and defeated the Governor's Magnet School in a computer skills contest.

Jerrie challenged me to excel when it came time for our college experience and our 30-year careers as educators. She is still challenging me every day.

SCHOOL-SPONSORED ACTIVITIES

During high school, most of my friends were involved in the same activities. Many of us participated in programs like One-Act Plays. Ingleside High School seemed to provide just enough of an experience to peak our interests in topics like theater. Over the years, Jerrie and I seldom miss an opportunity to support live theater in our community.

Dick and RW

Our high school annual yearbook was called 'The Mustang'. Many of our friends were on the yearbook staff. In my senior year, RW was the business manager for The Mustang and I was the Assistant Business Manager. That meant RW sold the advertisements and I took care of the paperwork and the money. Few could resist RW's sales pitch, and my newspaper account management experience made my job a fun sideline rather than a chore.

Over the years, RW shared many tales of his life in sales. RW once sold Bibles door to door. At one house, the homeowner ignored his smile and good humor and slammed the front door in his face. RW immediately ran to the back yard, made friends with the dog, and knocked loudly on the back door.

The man came to the door and RW said, "We need to talk."

The guy bought two Bibles.

Humble Compound Lighted Tennis Courts

Playing tennis with friends at the lighted tennis courts at the Humble Compound was a favorite activity. Ingleside High School had great tennis teams and tennis players. Some of us just enjoyed having a safe place to gather and compete without the rigor of another organized sport.

Jerrie played tennis for fun for at least fifty years after high school. I also enjoyed a friendly game of tennis for many years. We seem to have passed the love for the game on to a couple of our children. My daughter, Madonna, competed on the All-Navy tennis team during her first year in the Navy. She was like Jerry Lou Wright / Nix from Ingleside High School. She was a natural. My son, Joseph, was also an excellent tennis player. I hope he passes the love of the game on to his son, Joe Jr.

Little Bob's

Aransas Pass and Ingleside were small, neighboring Texas towns and our communities shared many special places. In addition to the youth centers, Aransas Pass had Little Bob's. I thought Little Bob's was the greatest drive-in eating establishment in the world. I know my world was limited to a small section of south Texas, but by the time I found out that Little Bob's closed, I had seen much of the world. I was still sure that a real part of America died.

At Little Bob's, we were welcome and our cars with their loud mufflers were welcome. The food was great, and the prices were affordable. The grown-ups just ignored us and enjoyed Little Bob's as much as we did.

Some change is good and necessary. Perhaps the closing of Little

Bob's was a sign of changing times. When this community landmark closed, I was probably at sea, on a ninety-day patrol, dreaming about having a great burger at Little Bob's while sitting in a cool car with my friends. I'm glad I have that time to remember. The news that Little Bob's had closed was as bad as the collapse of the Southwest Conference. At least as Ingleside Mustangs we can remember that the last Southwest Conference championship was won by Emory Bellard as the Head Coach of the Texas A&M Aggies.

REFLECTIONS OF A TEXAS TEENAGER – 1957

It was late at night and I was as free as any American kid could ever be as I drove my Oldsmobile through the countryside listening to XERF out of Del Rio, Texas. XERF was known as the Border Blaster radio station. AM 1570 was out of Ciudad Acuna, Coahuila, Mexico, which was just across the border from Del Rio, Texas. XERF could be heard across the United States and into Canada. They played mostly country music. "Walking After Midnight" by Patsy Cline was the kind of music I loved. I was also becoming a Rock and Roll fan. I particularly liked the country crossovers like Jerry Lee Lewis, Buddy Holly, and Elvis Presley.

Elvis came to Corpus Christi in 1957. I bought his concert tickets to impress my girlfriend, Jerrie. I would have preferred Jerry Lee Lewis or Buddy Holly, but Elvis was my only choice. At the concert, Elvis did not sound all that good to me. When I finally complained to Jerrie, she told me we were listening to the opening act. Elvis had not come on yet.

By then, I had already decided that I didn't like Rock n Roll concerts, the screaming crowd, the money for tickets. I would rather be in my car listening to the radio. I guess that it was good that I was a kid from the 1950s, rather than the 1960s. By the time the big concerts of the 1960s came around, I was chasing Commie Thugs on Fast Attack Nuclear Submarines. When my children were teenagers, I did not share my bias against Rock and Roll concerts. I believe they had a good time. Today, I go to listen to a local singer who sounds like Buddy Holly, but I am sure that it does not count as a concert.

In the evenings after the youth center closed, we would circle up at the parking lot at Jack Clark's Humble gas station and listen to music and tell stories. If the girls had not already been taken home, we might dance in the parking lot to anything from country music to Johnny Mathis singing *Send for Me* or Connie Francis singing *Who's Sorry Now*. We might also listen to what I called the New Orleans Rock 'n' Roll, Little Richard, Fats Domino, or Chuck Berry.

If we got too loud, our parents knew that the constable always came by to listen to the music and to make sure no one brought Lone Star Beer. It was a simple time and it was a fun time, but in my soul, I knew that it was decision time. I had to decide what I would do after high school graduation in May 1957.

DECISION TIME

When football season ended in my senior year of High School, I became consumed with the decision of what to do after graduation. I needed to decide.

Should I follow my childhood dream of joining the Navy like my Uncle Gene at the start of World War II? Should I try to continue my education in college and possibly even play football in college?

Dad did not support me in joining the military or going to college. The only overt support for college came from Grandpa Witte, Mr. Haugen my history teacher, coach, and mentor, and the new football coach, Coach Wagner.

For some of the kids, the future was clear. They would follow their parents. If their parents went from high school to college, they were expected to go to college, and probably to the same college. If a parent went to Texas A&M, they expected their kid to soon be an Aggie. If their parent had gone directly into the workforce, they probably would go directly to work in a similar skill.

I knew that was not for me. I did not know why, but I was not interested in being in the insurance business or working as an auto mechanic or a house painter. I appreciated my family helping me develop these skills and being willing to support me if I chose to go into those career fields. I simply knew that was not what I wanted.

In some families, the military was a tradition and was considered a patriotic duty, for at least one hitch. In my family, there was no consistent view of what I should do. I knew that Mom and Dad would support me if I made a thoughtful decision even if they disagreed with my decision.

I also needed to know what my girlfriend would think about my decision on what to do after high school. It was a different time and culture. Jerrie Swinney and I were inseparable. To help answer this question, I turned to the ultimate source of family wisdom, Granny.

I asked her, "Granny, what should I do after high school?"

Granny said, "Let's go fishing."

I asked Leon Taylor, my high school principal, "Mr. Taylor, What would happen if I took a day out of school and took Granny fishing?"

He responded, "Knowing you, you'll get sunburned since you never wear a hat. It's only a problem when you slip out of school. Check with your teachers for assignments and we will call it family business."

I thought *this is much easier than climbing out the Study Hall window.*

FISHING FOR A DECISION WITH GRANNY

I knew Granny was ready for a fishing trip. She had not been herself since Grandad passed and she lost her home. We decided to go to the pier at Port Aransas. Mom and Dad thought it was a great idea since Leon approved and they knew that both Granny and I needed time away from family and time together. Neither of us had been ourselves lately.

I was tight with a dollar, but I knew this was going to be an important day. I took Granny to breakfast at the Bakery Café in

Aransas Pass. Breakfast out was a real treat for Granny. She was always the cook and server, not the person being served. She liked their biscuits, served with local honey. We both had eggs over easy and bacon. We cleaned our plates. Granny made a profound assessment.

"We are going to have a good day. Put on your hat so you don't get sunburned. You have Gene's face."

When we got to the pier, Granny made her next speech, "I'll fish for sheepshead today. Put my stool right here. You can fish for whatever you want. Thank you for breakfast."

That was the longest statement I ever heard Granny make. It was by far, the longest statement she made all day.

How am I going to solve my problem if Granny will not talk? Oh well, I love being on the saltwater, I must have saltwater in my veins. Good Grief! A profound insight already and Granny has not said a word.

About two hours later, I finally asked the big question again.

"Granny, what should I do after high school?"

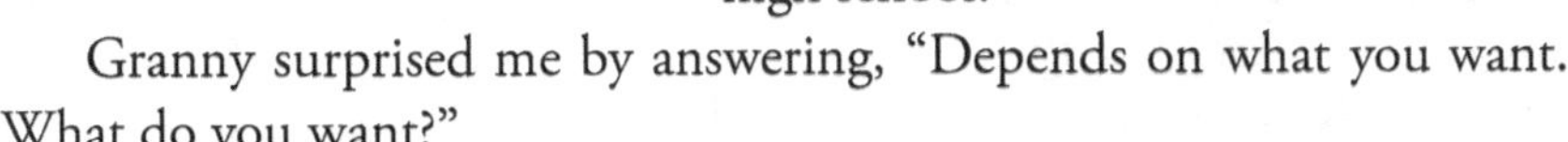

| Granny fishing

Granny surprised me by answering, "Depends on what you want. What do you want?"

I thought for a while and then started to speak.

Granny said, "Shush, you will scare the fish, tell me on the way home."

I thought to myself, *what does she want me to do, just sit here fishing in the quiet and figure out what I want?*

And I did. I love Granny. She always had the answer.

For lunch, we had fried mashed potato sandwiches as only Granny could make. They were wonderful and they were the last ones I ever ate.

We caught a nice mess of sheepshead. Granny preferred

sheepshead. She loved the bony fish from both freshwater and saltwater. She loved taking her time, picking them out.

On the way home, Granny said, "So?"

I said, "Granny, I know what I'm looking for after high school, but I'm not sure what I'm going to do. I could join the military and begin doing what I want right away, or I could go to college first and then join the military."

I told Granny what I was looking for.

- I wanted some excitement.
- I wanted to do dangerous and important work.
- I wanted to be independent.
- I wanted to leave Ingleside, Texas, at least for a while.
- I wanted a life on or near the ocean but doing more than fishing.
- I wanted to see the world outside of Texas, and I wanted to see it with my girlfriend, Jerrie.

I asked Granny to keep all of this between us for now. I said, "I will need to leave Ingleside for at least a while."

Granny said, "I know."

When I told Granny, "I do not think that I am going to make many folks happy," Granny said, "I know."

I think that in the quiet of the day, on the saltwater, fishing for sheepshead, Granny also came to know about her life without Grandad. She did not share that with me, but I think if she had, I could have truthfully said, "I know."

After Grandad passed, Granny lost what was important to her, except the love of her family. She lost her home in Beeville. When she lost her home, she lost her independence and the place where she practiced her crafts and the activities that occupied her life. Granny no longer had a place. PW was gone and many members of the family had moved away from home to begin their lives as adults, including the first generation of her grandchildren and her son, Gene. In some ways, perhaps Granny felt that getting her grandchildren, Ruth, Patricia, Pete, and I started in life was her last major project.

Ruth went to college and began a successful career, Patricia found happiness in marriage, Pete found his independence although his life was cut short, and Granny helped me make my decision about my career after high school.

The year after I joined the Navy, my beloved Granny passed and went straight to Heaven.

DECIDING BETWEEN COLLEGE AND THE MILITARY

Coach Haugen's support for higher education was not as well received by parents as his coaching and teaching skills. Mostly we were a small community of hard-working folks. The parents who wanted a college education for their children could afford it and the others viewed college as work preparation that was not needed. Many good jobs were available at the Reynolds Aluminum Plant, the local chemical companies, the refineries, and in the oil fields.

When Coach Haugen approached Dad in my junior year, Dad repeated the well-worn phrase that he used whenever college was mentioned. He said, "I had a college guy working for me once and he was not worth a plug nickel." For me, that ended the conversation, but Coach Haugen was persistent.

When I was a senior, Coach sent me to visit Texas Lutheran College, his alma mater. While at Texas Lutheran, I would apply for admission and a scholarship, and try out for the football team. I participated in spring football drills and stayed in the dorm for several days. I also took a battery of academic tests. I think Coach Haugen sent me to Texas Lutheran because he was sure that the decision about going to college or joining the Navy was weighing on me. He knew that at Texas Lutheran I would get the information I needed to make a decision that was best for me. Texas Lutheran was, and still is, a private Liberal Arts College where academic excellence was the primary emphasis and sports were secondary.

On the football field, I held my own, but I was a boy among men. Many of the football players were military veterans going to school on the G.I. Bill. I accepted that in football, I was a good player and a hardworking teammate, but I was not a great football player. If I went to college and played football, I needed to go to a small college where I could play and enjoy the game. During my stay at Texas Lutheran, I went to town with several guys from the football team. One of the guys that I seemed to have a special connection with really intrigued me. Leonard was a sophomore and an honor roll student.

When I asked him if he had been an honor roll student in high school, he said, "No, I was just an average student. I loved school and I had great friends. I was good at sports, but I only made average grades. I was excited to finish school and get on with life. I wanted some action and I wanted to see if I could be successful without the help of my parents. I loved my parents, but I wanted to make my own decisions for a while."

I kept asking Leonard questions. "So, what did you do?"

Leonard provided me with a summary of his perspective on life after high school.

"I joined the Marines and I grew up. I became a Marine. I will always be a Marine, no matter what else I do. As a Marine, I became independent from my parents. While I was in Korea, I finally learned what our coaches had been trying to teach us in high school sports. All for one and one for all is the most important lesson in sports. I survived some hard times. While it's great to try and be independent, life is a team sport and sometimes your life is in the hands of your teammates. The sport changes but the need to be a team player never changes. In the Marines, your teammates need to depend on you, and you are dependent on them. It is a tougher game than football, but the team concept is the same. If you are not a good teammate, you are not a good player."

Leonard suggested that kids come to college from high school trying to be independent of their parents and to have a good time while they are learning to survive without the help of their parents. If they don't find a strong peer group to replace their parents, their effort at independence usually results in not putting in the time and effort needed to be successful in college. They often fail or find that they have a steep hill to climb before they can be successful.

Leonard said, "All I need to do is focus on my academic work. I play football for fun and the school and my teammates. I am a Marine and being a good teammate is second nature to me. I'm smart, I'm a good football player and I survived Korea. I'll excel at college and I'll be successful in a career."

I thought, *Good Grief, Leonard, you could be a preacher or a Marine Recruiter.* I asked Leonard if he was talking or his Lone Star Beer?

He said, "It's the absolute truth. It's as true for you as it is for me. Your coach would not have sent you up here unless you were smart enough to be anything you want. It's your job to figure out the best way for you to get started."

I said to myself, "I'm going home and join the Marines."

I almost did.

I realized after our discussions that night, that the decision to go to college did not necessarily need to be made at the end of high school. I also would learn that it takes a team of folks to make good decisions. I'd not talked to all the folks I would need to talk to if I were going to make a good career or college decision. Many of the guys who would have been my teammates at Texas Lutheran College were at least four years older than me. They had put college off after high school, invested four years in the real world, and now had the G.I. Bill to help with their college expenses. When I left Texas Lutheran College, I guessed that the G.I. Bill was probably how Coach Haugen had attended Texas Lutheran College.

I received a tuition offer from Texas Lutheran. I must have had good test scores on their exams because I did not have exceptional grades. This offer was probably worth quite a bit of money at a private school, but it would have been difficult for me without other financial help. Federal Financial Aid as we know it today did not exist in the 1950s.

Coach Haugen also set up for me to go to Southwest Texas State College, now Texas State University, to try out for a football scholarship. I was accepted to the college, and after football spring training, I was provided an opportunity to be a walk-on for the football team with the hope of earning a full scholarship. Dad said that meant they needed a blocking dummy. My Uncle Gene worked at

Southwest Texas State and offered to let me stay with him and his wife, Alene until I was able to earn a full scholarship. I was not too excited about the life of a "walk-on" football player and blocking dummy.

The two men I respected most besides Dad, had served in the military and then went to college on the G.I. Bill. If that route was good enough for them, I was beginning to think it would be good enough for me. Dad was probably right about the whole *plug nickel* thing.

Coach Wagner, the new Football Coach at Ingleside High School, also encouraged me to consider college.

He said, "You're smart enough for college and you're a good football player. You would do well at a small college. Let me test the waters and see how I can help."

By the time Coach came to tell me that he had been notified of a full scholarship for me at a small college out in West Texas, Sul Ross State College, his alma mater, I had already joined the military. I feel honored that my coaches would want me to go to their alma mater. I do follow Texas Lutheran sports and. I keep thinking I will go and visit Sul Ross to see what might have been home for a few years. I cannot imagine a better place for me to grow up than serving in the military. I was ready for some action.

After I visited Texas Lutheran College and my pivotal conversation with Leonard, I came home with the belief that I should postpone college until after I had served one hitch in the military. I was so impressed with Leonard and his Marine Corp stories that I briefly thought that I should join the Marine Corp, rather than following my Uncle Gene into the Navy. Being a sailor like my Uncle Gene had been a dream since he came home from World War II in his sailor suit. After I decided to join the military, I also decided that I should join soon after high school graduation. A lot of effort had been made to help me make a good decision between college and the military and I did not want to get distracted. I needed closure.

On my first visit to the recruiters in Corpus Christi, I only visited the Marine Corp Recruiter and the Navy Recruiter. The Marine at the Marine Corps Recruiting Office was much more impressive than the Sailor at the Navy Recruiting Office. He was spit and polish and the

Navy Recruiter did not look anything like my Uncle Gene in starched whites or bell-bottoms. The Marine said that with my hunting experience and knowledge of guns, I would love the Marine Corp. All the Navy Recruiter wanted to talk about was that, with two years of algebra, and a year of geometry, I would probably qualify for an Electronic Rating and get a great education.

I thought *I want action. I've decided to pass on education for now. I'll probably go to college on the GI Bill after a hitch in the military.* I signed a Letter of Intent with the Marine Recruiter with no additional research.

I did not think that Dad would care about which service I joined because he did not want me to join the military. Dad and I had already had the military conversation, and he agreed to be supportive of my decision to join the military. Dad was upset that I made a spur of the moment decision with the Marine Recruiter after years of dreaming about being a sailor like my Uncle Gene. He called his boss, friend, and Navy veteran Joe Hunt, and asked him to talk to me.

| Joe Hunt and Dick

Joe arrived in less than an hour and our conversation lasted until after midnight. Joe never said a word about the Marines. Joe told me sea stories about his adventures in the Navy. He suggested that my love of being on the water with him and Dad made the Navy my natural choice. We discussed everything from small boats to submarines and even battleships. I had no idea that Joe Hunt, whom I fished with and went shrimping with had a complete life of experiences on oceans all over the world. He also said that while college might be in my future, the Navy was at the forefront of a new wave of technology. With electronics training, I might even get to serve on a nuclear submarine like the USS Nautilus (SSN-571). Joe seemed to have an almost encyclopedic knowledge of the US Navy.

I soon found out that Joe Hunt was not without influence. I received what seemed to me to be special treatment, as a variety of active duty and retired officers and senior enlisted men shared their Navy experiences with me.

My letter of intent with the Marine Corp was withdrawn. I began the process of enlisting in the Navy with several recommendations for advanced technical training and Submarine School. I was swept away with the attention of new friends who seemed like family. These new friends had histories that I never imagined. I wondered about the Marine Corps, but in Navy Boot Camp, I found out that I was about as good at marching as I was at typing or playing the piano. I knew that I was moving in the right direction by joining the US Navy. I had sea legs, not marching legs. It would be Anchors Away for me. If I made it to Submarine School, I would trade the sound of my glasspack mufflers for the rumble of sixteen-cylinder GMC diesel engines on a fleet type submarine, and then the quiet power of nuclear attack submarines. Eventually, I would help build and put to sea the submarine that is the most decorated ship in Naval History.

6

THE UNITED STATES NAVY

1957 THROUGH 1958

The love of my life, Jerrie Swinney, and my father took me to Jack Clark's Humble Gas Station to catch the Greyhound Bus. I was on my way to Houston, Texas, to begin the process of enlisting in the U.S. Navy.

HOUSTON, TEXAS – SWEARING IN

To that point in my life, I considered myself well-traveled, although I had never been to a big city like Houston, Texas. My world consisted of an area of the South Texas Gulf Coast bordered on the north by Victoria, Texas and the Matagorda Bay, on the west by Beeville, Texas, and on the south and east by the Corpus Christi area, (known then, and now to locals as Corpus). Corpus included the small towns and islands that bordered the Corpus Christi Bay and the Gulf of Mexico. If you drew a circle of my area, I roamed freely in an area with a radius of about sixty miles.

When I was a child of seven, I left the state of Texas on one occasion to accompany my cousins, Ruth and Patricia Morrow, when they traveled to Ringgold, Louisiana to welcome their dad, my Uncle

Billy, home from WWII. I had also traveled to San Antonio, Texas to see Gene Autry, the Alamo, and to visit a great aunt. This trip to San Antonio was my only big city experience. San Antonio was not that big, but it was big enough that Dad said we should avoid it like the plague. In the spring of 1957, I had gone up north, almost to Austin, when I visited San Marcos, Texas, the home of Southwest Texas State College (now Texas State), and Seguin, Texas, to visit Texas Lutheran College.

I had been visiting these two schools to participate in Spring Training for their football programs, academic testing, and the admissions process.

I liked both Seguin and San Marcos, but I knew they were not real cities, just bigger than Ingleside.

By the time I got off the bus in Houston, we had picked up six additional small-town kids who were headed for the Armed Forces Processing Center. A burly sailor who looked nothing like my Uncle Gene, or even my recruiter in Corpus, met us at the bus and called out our names. He gave each of us an envelope that contained coupons for a night in a local hotel that was near the bus station and meal tickets for a café that was on the first floor of the hotel.

When I saw the hotel, I was sure it was flea-infested, but I managed to sleep the night. I was already somewhat homesick for my small hometown. This place had some seedy characters hanging around. In Ingleside, I knew all the seedy-looking characters. I probably knew their whole families and they were mostly seedy-looking because they worked hard in some hot and dirty place to earn a living, not because they were dangerous. Two kids from Victoria, a big town compared to Ingleside, said not to worry about the seedy characters, we were safe.

When I was ready to cash in my breakfast coupon, I had more surprises. The waitress asked how I wanted my eggs, scrambled, over easy, sunnyside, or hard. At home, there was no choice. It was either fried or scrambled, depending on what Mom chose to cook. I told the waitress, scrambled because I thought that would be a safe choice. I wasn't sure just how well done some of the other choices would be. At our house, even poached eggs were well done. The breakfast came with eggs, toast, and what looked like Cream of Wheat, although it was sort of coarse. I asked the waitress what was wrong with my Cream of Wheat.

She said, "Honey, that's not Cream of Wheat. That's grits! You're from Texas and you don't know about grits?"

I was taken aback! I had heard of grits, but we did not eat them at my house. I had never even seen them. Dad said he had eaten a trainload of grits during the Depression, and they were not allowed in our house. It looked like I had a lot to learn.

The guys at the Armed Forces Processing Center were a lot grumpier and bossier than my recruiter. They certainly didn't look anything like my Uncle Gene with his white hat on the back of his head.

First Train Ride

When we were finished processing, we were sworn in (no turning back now) and put on a passenger train to San Diego, California to attend Boot Camp. I had never been on a train. I had never been to West Texas, New Mexico, Arizona, or California. I had never seen a mountain. I was excited about the places I would see in the next couple of days. Perhaps the recruiter was right. I had joined the Navy and I would see the world. Also, for this trip, I was excited about the train ride.

Jerrie's Uncle Bubba had regaled me with stories about how he had hopped a freight out of faraway places like Santa Barbara, California, and Topeka, Kansas. The only negative I could see about the trip was the warning from the Processing Center to not get off the train at any of its stops. Even though I still didn't have a white hat, I was in the Navy and if I missed the train along the way when it pulled out, I would be thrown in the brig, whatever that was. I would just see these new places from the window of the train.

I was beginning to like the idea of someone other than Mom cooking for me. I had never eaten in a real restaurant. In Corpus, we had the world's first Whataburger Stand, where you could get a huge hamburger and a tub of root beer. In Ingleside, we had The Chili Place and Mr. Lyles' Hamburger Joint. In Aransas Pass, we had the Bakery Café where I sometimes got to eat breakfast when I was going fishing or hunting with Dad and my uncles. We also had Little Bob's. But to me, Little Bob's was a Drive-In. I never went in and sat down in Little Bob's. The only real sit-down experience other than the Bakery Café was if Dad could be talked into Sunday dinner at the Taco Shack after church on Sunday. For $3.00 you could get a belly-busting Mexican plate. Formal Sunday dinner at home after we left Beeville and the Grand Old House seemed to end our family tradition for a sit-down Sunday Dinner. Jerrie and I have attempted to re-establish the family tradition of Sunday Dinner.

On the train, I got to sit down and order every meal. I loved the train ride. We had meals served by a waiter while viewing mountains out the window. It was nice while it lasted.

BOOT CAMP – A NEW TEAM

Boot Camp was an eye-opener. The first day, I was herded from one place to another. I was issued my new uniforms that didn't fit. I got my ducktail haircut shaved off. I got a shot in every place you could put a shot. But after comparing notes from Uncle Bubba (Army, WWII), and my Uncle Billy (Army, WWII), I knew I was getting off light. They said that the Navy Boot Camp was soft compared to the Army.

Once we were assigned to our Boot Camp Company, things were much better. We had about thirty guys in our company. Our Company Commander was a salty First-Class Petty Officer named Butch Carvallo. We marched everywhere and some of us were given jobs, such as Recruit Company Commander, Yeoman, and Squad Leader. These jobs were somewhat temporary and would come and go as you either excelled or screwed up. I liked Boot Camp, or at least most of it. I compared it to South Texas two-a-day football practice in August when the temperature was over 100 degrees and the humidity was over 100 percent. But the coaches were right there with you, and Butch was right there with us during Boot Camp. Butch was the coach and Boot Camp was just a new team. We had to learn the Navy's rules and we also had to learn Butch's rules.

There was a lot to learn. Coach Butch wanted us to win Best Company in addition to Best Everything You Could Think of from Cleanest Barracks to Best Marching Squad. I understood trying to win and was good with that part of Boot Camp.

I did not like the huge group showers with strangers. The guys in the showers had too many funny wisecracks to suit me. We had the group showers in high school sports, but I knew those guys and I knew that if any of them did anything funny, they would answer to the Coach, and somebody would call their mom. No one tried anything funny in the showers at Boot Camp, but I still never liked it.

I did not like the sleeping arrangements. I slept in the garage at home but at least I had a double bed. There were no double beds in Boot Camp, only bunk beds with semi grown men making all sorts of night sounds and one who even walked in his sleep. I got a bottom bunk, but I still didn't like the idea of people sleeping above me, and on both sides of me. I would have a lot to learn about sleeping arrangements when I finally made it to a ship and then a submarine!

Boot Camp was like two-a-day practices in August, it was sometimes a love-hate relationship; I slimmed up and I decided that I was going to like the Navy. It was another team and I liked being on teams. I did not excel at anything in Boot Camp, except a few of the academic classes, but I was never in serious trouble either. Like high school sports and high school academics, I was never a star, but I was a good team player and a good student.

I liked my new coach, Petty Officer Butch Carvallo, and he seemed to like me. Butch and his wife Florence and their many kids would become close family friends.

When I returned home to Ingleside, Mom said I was a close image of my Uncle Gene when he had on his dress whites and white sailor hat. The Bear had shed thirty pounds and was proud to sport his Seaman Apprentice Stripes. I was excited about orders to Sonar School in San Diego CA. I was not exactly sure what sonar was, but Butch said that it was a special school and you only went to that school if you had good math and science scores, good hearing and if your security clearance showed that you had never been in any kind of trouble with the law. Goodness knows that was true. If I ever got into trouble in Ingleside, our Constable would call Mom, or Dad, or both, and I would have been grounded. I was excited about Sonar School and beginning my Navy career and my life as a married man. Jerrie, my new wife, would be heading to San Diego with me. We would both be beginning the process of separating from our parents, a necessary part of our growing up. We hoped the military would be a good place to begin that process.

THE HITCH-HIKING PLAN

The plan was that I would go to California, check in to Fleet Sonar School, and find an apartment. Jerrie would come to California when we had an apartment. We would sell the hot-rod Oldsmobile and get us a more traditional car when we could afford it. In the meantime, I would find an apartment on the city bus line and take the city bus to work each day. I was fascinated with Uncle Bubba's stories of hitch-hiking around the country. I broached the idea of hitch-hiking to San Diego and Dad was the first one to respond. He said, "I always wanted to hitch-hike somewhere, and I never got around to it."

Dad and I planned my route together. We would put my seabag on the Greyhound bus to San Diego at Jack Clark's Humble Service Station. Dad and Jerrie would take me to Sinton. We would have breakfast at our favorite café on the outskirts of Sinton and I would walk across the street after breakfast and begin hitchhiking on Highway 181.

Highway 181 would take me to San Antonio through Beeville. From San Antonio, I would catch a ride on Highway 90 through El Paso, New Mexico, and Arizona to San Diego. We were sure the plan would work. In the 1950s, everyone stopped to give military men in uniform a ride, and hitchhiking was common.

When I got to San Diego, I could call Butch Carvallo. Butch and his wife Florence had already adopted us. Butch said that now that he was no longer my Company Commander, we were just a couple of sailors. He said, "I'll be your Sea Daddy." I was good with Sea Daddy. I was about to leave Dad in Texas.

Jerrie and Dad sat in the car at the café while I walked across the road in my whites with my hat on the back of my head. I hoped that I looked like the sailor pictures of my Uncle Gene.

Jerrie said, "You look good, sailor. I love you and take care of yourself." She said that to me every time I left her for the next twenty-one years of Navy life.

I must have looked okay because I was picked up by a couple, Dan and Mary from Kerrville, within five minutes. They would be going through San Antonio on their way home. They had spent a week in Port Aransas where Dan had gone deep sea fishing while Mary worked on her tan in front of the cottage they had rented.

Dan had been a parachute rigger during his hitch in the Navy and had been stationed at Chase Field in Beeville. He had hitchhiked home to Kerrville on this same road many times. Dan and Mary seemed to be a little more affluent than my family. Dan went deep-sea fishing on a charter boat when they went to Port Aransas, and they always rented an oceanfront cottage.

We never rented a cottage at Port Aransas. We stayed on the beach. The closest Dad came to deep-sea fishing was when he drifted into the Gulf in his bay fishing boat. The second time this happened, the Coast Guard said, "This is the last time we're dragging you home."

Dan's previous hitch-hiking experience came in handy. He said, "Because San Antonio is an Air Force town, the Air Force has established several stations with signs that say: *Give A Service Man A Lift.*" Dan took me to one of these stations, on the west side of San Antonio, on Highway 90, after buying me lunch. Dan and Mary gave me their address and phone number.

It was a different time in America. I remembered the kindness of Dan and Mary when I saw servicemen treated differently a few years later.

I waited no more than ten minutes on Highway 90 when George stopped and gave me a lift. He said, "How are far are you going?"

I said, "I'm going to San Diego, California." He asked me if I was an experienced driver.

I said, "I've driven everything from hot rods to grain trucks. Why?"

He said, "I'm on my way to San Diego, and if we can share the driving, we could drive straight through. If you could help with the gas, that would be even better." I agreed. Dad had given me his Texaco Credit Card and said he thought it would come in handy.

George had completed a four-year hitch in the Air Force. He was an aircraft mechanic. This would be his second trip to San Diego. He interviewed for a job at one of the aircraft plants in San Diego and was on his way back to begin his new job.

Uncle Bubba was right about hitchhiking. This was exciting. I changed into jeans and a T-shirt at a truck stop. George and I rolled up the miles. In West Texas, New Mexico, and Arizona we seldom saw another car. It was a great trip. We ate hamburgers at truck stops, drank coffee, and took turns sleeping and driving. George's car was a 1955 Chevrolet, with one of Chevrolet's new V8 engines. I thought *driving a car without loud mufflers would be O.K. if I could drive a car like this.*

My only driving concern came when my last shift was to drive through the mountains just before San Diego. I had never driven in hills, much less mountains. I tried to pretend that I was in one of the cross-country races I had read about. If we had been in a race, we would have lost. The road had hairpin curves and thousand-foot drop-offs with long downhill high-speed runs. It was exciting but scary. I managed to get myself, George, and his car, back to flatland before George took over to drive us into San Diego.

We had lunch at a café near George's new job, less than 24 hours after he gave me a lift. I changed back into my uniform and gave George the address of the Fleet Sonar School. It turned out to be just a few miles down the road.

Fleet Sonar School

I checked in at Fleet Sonar School and had a bunk, locker, and a pass to the mess hall before nightfall. The barracks Master at Arms, (MAA), said I would be able to sleep in the next day. It was Sunday, and there was no muster. The base was small and laid back compared to the base where I had boot camp.

I used the payphone to check in with Jerrie, Mom and Dad, and even Butch, my Sea Daddy. I slept for twelve hours and then had a good breakfast at the mess hall.

My plan for Sunday was to catch a bus to downtown San Diego, rent a locker at a locker club, pick up my seabag at the bus station, and return to the base.

I did not need the bus until I got to the foot of Broadway in downtown San Diego, (Fleet Landing). There were always folks willing to give you a ride from the base to Fleet Landing. I rented a locker at a locker club, just across the street from Fleet Landing.

We had to leave the base in uniform. We would change into civvies (civilian clothes), either at home or at a locker club. I had no home, so I needed a locker club. I unpacked my seabag and put my civilian clothes, two pair of Levi's, my cowboy boots, a dress shirt for church, and a pair of tennis shoes into my locker. Then I returned to the base and packed that locker with my Navy Uniforms. I even ironed a dungaree shirt to make a good impression the next morning.

The Barracks MAA was a third-class petty officer who was also waiting for his class to start. He warned me that, until class started, I would be working for Base Maintenance.

He also warned me, "Your chief is real A........."

I said, "He can't be that bad."

He said, "Yes, he can."

He was.

We were up at 6:00 am and mustered at 7:00 am. I wasn't worried. I had a great breakfast. I never met a coach, teacher, or boss that I could not make friends with. I also had never met Chief Underwood. Everyone else called him Chief U or Chief U Who. I came to call him much worse, but only under my breath.

I called my Sea Daddy. Butch checked him out and told me that Chief U had been transferred to the school as an instructor but was now the permanent chief in charge of the transients waiting for school. Butch's advice was to make a good impression at your work assignment, and they will ask for you to be assigned to them until school starts.

That advice served me well and limited my time with Chief U to morning muster on most days.

My assignment was to the base bowling alley. This was another first. I had never seen a bowling alley. I learned to set pins, clean the alleys, clean the heads, and scrub the toilets. I volunteered to do anything else that was needed. To me, it was just work and another team. I liked being a teammate and I loved the bowling alley. I worked hard, and I became a regular worker at the bowling alley.

I also had my first legal beer at the bowling alley. On base, we could drink at age 18. They did not have Lone Star, Shiner, Falstaff, or Pearl beer. This was not Texas. I decided to follow the advice of Grandad, PW Morrow, "Any beer will work in a pinch." I stuck to Schlitz, Budweiser, or Miller High Life since I had heard of them. On several occasions, I could have easily had a few too many beers, at ten cents a can, but I didn't want to do anything to impact my job.

On days that I was not in trouble with Chief U, I would go to the foot of Broadway, change clothes at the locker club and take the bus up Broadway until I reached the area where there were apartments for rent.

THE SLUM APARTMENT

I knew I needed to get an apartment on the bus route. I knew nothing about living in a city. I rented a small apartment in a large old house that looked much like the grand old house in Beeville. Jerrie came out to San Diego and we set up housekeeping.

The apartment was okay, but for a couple of Texas kids, shopping was almost impossible without a car. There was one small neighborhood store. It was a friendly place, and we could get milk, bread, eggs, rice, dried beans, and a chunk of salt pork. The neighbors did not seem to visit very much, and some of the men seemed to hang around rather than go to work. Jerrie visited with one of the ladies who lived in the next apartment. Her husband would have qualified as a seedy character if he lived in Ingleside.

When the first of the month came, the military allotment did not show up. We were frantic. There was no other source of money for the rent. I had not been following Grandpa Witte's "Enough is Enough" plan.

About three days after everyone else had received their allotment, the lady that Jerrie visited with came over with Jerrie's check. Her husband, the seedy character, had stolen it from our mailbox. He was not smart enough to figure a way to cash the check. The lady begged, and Jerrie agreed to not call the police.

After another three days, a television crew showed up. Everyone looked seedy, except the cameramen. They were shooting a scene from a TV police drama. The main character was a 'down on her luck' prostitute. I did not know what a police drama was since we did not have a TV. I knew what a prostitute was. We began looking for a new apartment.

ADULTS ONLY

One of my instructors was a local boy. He said, "You need to move closer to downtown. Let me call my grandmother. She lives in a nice apartment on 17th Street. She doesn't have a car and she can walk everywhere she needs to go. It is a safe area. I believe her apartment complex is restricted to old folks, but she knows the area and can help you."

Her apartment complex was nice, and although only older folks lived there, it was not restricted to seniors. It was an Adults Only complex. We were teenagers, but because we were married, we qualified as adults.

We liked the grandmother. She and several of her neighbors liked us and they seemed to be the power brokers at the apartment complex. It was decided, after intensive cross-examination over coffee, milk, and cake that we would be a safe novelty to add to their residents list.

The only apartment available was a nice studio apartment. It was great for us because we didn't have any furniture.

THE BEAST

With the move, we decided we needed a car. We needed to visit Butch and Florence. We needed to go to the Commissary. We needed to find the Navy Hospital. We knew we needed a different kind of car. We were now officially adults. We needed a grown-up car, not a hot rod.

I called Herbert. Dad gave me the inside story on how to find a dependable and cheap car that I would have the skills to maintain. I knew that would mean no high compression overhead-valve, V-8 engines.

I found a 1946 Pontiac, four-door sedan with a straight-eight engine. I knew this kind of car. Dad, the mechanic, was a fan of straight-eight engines. He said they did not get broken in until they had at least 100,000 miles.

This car was truly ugly, which made it affordable. It was that maroon color that turns to white powder after a few years. The car had been sitting up, outside, for a long time. It only had 70,000 miles on the odometer. The engine sounded terrible. While I had no desire to be an auto mechanic or a painter, I had those skills thanks to Dad and my uncles.

I called Dad and gave him my assessment of the Pontiac. We agreed that the engine probably had sticking valves, a common problem on the old straight eights when they were not driven. I also told him that the engine oil and transmission fluid in the Hydra-Matic transmission was clean. I was not able to check the rear end grease. The points and plugs had not been changed in years. Dad asked me to do one more check. The owner let me pull each wheel and look at the wheel bearings and brakes. We were soon the proud owners of the ugliest car on earth, and it did not run very well either. We named her the Beast.

Dad registered the Beast in Texas. This was a perk for the military. We could register our cars in our home state. Mrs. Robinson, our insurance agent in Ingleside, transferred the insurance from the hot rod.

The old folks at our apartment complex probably doubted their decision to share their home with a couple of teenagers when they saw the Beast, but Dad and I had been correct. The Beast just needed some loving care and a paint job.

The Transformation to Old Blue

I ran a can of Casite through the engine on the first tank of gas, changed the points and plugs, and set the timing. The Beast purred like a kitten. The sticking valves were taken care of and every cylinder had good compression and fire. Jerrie used her cleaning magic on the inside of the car, with finger-pointing and good ideas from the other ladies at our apartment. When they finished, the inside of the Pontiac looked new. We sanded and sealed the old paint and did not find a ding or dent.

When we finished painting The Beast, it was a beautiful baby blue. The old folks in the apartment complex came to view the transformation. They recommended we change the name from the Beast to Old Blue. Old Blue gave many of our neighbors, who were without transportation except for the city bus, a ride anywhere they needed to go.

We were proud of our skills and our roots. We were Texas kids. We needed a car and we took care of business. Grandpa Witte would have given his blessing. Old Blue met the Enough criteria.

SAN DIEGO, A WONDERLAND

Although we now had transportation, our entertainment was walking up and down Broadway. San Diego was a wonderland of cafés and shops. We began to collect household items. Many of these items came from the Salvation Army store or the Goodwill store. We had not known that such places even existed. The stores were nice, and the workers were nice to us. Before long we even had a television. The television worked with tiny rabbit ears, rather than the tower antennas needed in Ingleside.

We became attached to the folks at our apartment complex. I think they came to value us. We dreaded the day we would have to leave our new friends. We had established a home and we felt the comfort of being at home in our little apartment. Soon, we would be transferred to Submarine School in Connecticut.

Many of our neighbors ate their main meal out every day, and they opened our eyes to new culinary delights. We had never seen or heard of a Pizza Pie. Just down the street was Mona Lisa Pizza. When we took our evening walk, we would watch the chef at Mona Lisa Pizza. He would toss a pizza into the air and look out at us as we stood watching in amazement. We did this every night for two weeks until payday. On payday, we went to Mona Lisa Pizza for our first Pizza Pie. The chef told us we had entertained him for two weeks, and our first pizza was on the house. We told him he would have to tell us what to order. He gave us an education and our first pizza. Over sixty years later, San Diego still has a Mona Lisa Pizza.

When we went back to Texas, Jerrie was a superstar when she made our families their first Pizza Pie.

Our other favorite eating place was the Blue-Plate Special Café. Our favorite item on the menu was the Blue Plate Special. We ate at home every night as kids, so we understood the concept. This café had a different special every day. We studied the menu with great excitement. We did one eat out each week. One week it was Mona Lisa Pizza and the next week it was the Blue Plate Special. Planning and budgeting were critical.

God's Blessing

I settled in at Fleet Sonar School. Like high school, I was in the middle of the pack. I worried that, because I was not at the top of the class, I might not be assigned to Submarine School. As it turned out, many of my classmates were either afraid of submarines or had some issues with security or hearing. Surface sonar used active transmissions to reflect sound waves off a target much like radar. Submarines used primarily passive sonar which was a focus on listening for specific and unique low-level sounds. God had blessed me with hearing skills that were much like speed for a runner. You either had it or you didn't. Those skills served me well for a full career.

I received orders to submarine school. I was never sure if it was my hearing, my recommendations from my instructors and my navy veteran friends, the fact that I had no security issues, or the fact that I had three years of Algebra and Geometry in high school. Perhaps it was all or none of these reasons. The US Navy made the correct decision. I was good for the submarine force and it was good for me and my family. We were ready for a new adventure.

It was an adventure!

First Sea Story

I had been in school for almost eighteen months including Sonar School and Submarine School. I had seen a good bit of the United States. I hadn't been a crew member on a submarine or any other ship. I didn't consider myself a real sailor. I was not salty, and I was not a sub sailor.

When I completed Submarine School in New London, Connecticut, I received orders back to San Diego, California for duty on the USS Capitaine (SS-336). Assuming that my submarine would be in San Diego, California, Jerrie and I drove from Connecticut back home to Texas and then to San Diego, California where we found a nice, but tiny, backyard apartment on Texas Street. (Naturally).

The adventure of leaving San Diego after Sonar School, driving to Texas and then to Connecticut for Submarine School, and then returning to San Diego to catch my submarine was a real adventure. This is a story that I will share in my next memoir (Sub Sailor).

When I reported to the Submarine Squadron in San Diego, I was told that my submarine had already deployed, and I would be flying to the Western Pacific to catch my submarine. I started to ask if they could just send me to another submarine, but I'm glad that I didn't. The next few months would be one of the great adventures of my life.

First Airplane Ride

I flew out of Lindbergh Field in San Diego on my first ride in an airplane. It was a large four-engine prop-driven airliner. We flew from San Diego to Honolulu, Hawaii, and then to Tokyo, Japan with a stop at Midway Island.

While I am a white-knuckle flyer nowadays, that initial episode was so exciting that I felt no fear. The Navy posters were correct. I was going to see the world or at least the Western Pacific.

And I did.

The pilot prepared us for Midway Island when he informed us that our landing would be escorted by a squadron of Goony Birds. The birds lined up on each wingtip and landed with us. Midway was small, but I thought, *I'm glad I came to Midway Island; this visit gives perspective to my World War II History Studies.* When we got off the plane, there was only a small terminal with snacks and facilities to gas up the plane. Midway was good for a small-town kid. Nothing prepared me for Tokyo, not even Houston.

My orders said to travel from Tokyo to Yokosuka, Japan as directed by available government transportation. While I am sure that I still had a bit of small-town expectation, I sort of envisioned a Navy van with a guy holding up a sign saying, Seaman Witte. Lots of luck with that! There were mobs of people and very few who spoke English and even fewer who seemed in the least interested in helping a kid in an American sailor suit. Eventually, I was directed to an area where I could retrieve my sea bag.

GUARDIAN ANGEL

Then, out of nowhere, a guardian angel appeared in the form of a Japanese man about the age of Dad.

He said, in perfect English "Hey kid, you, sailor, you going to Yokosuka?"

I said, "Yes, I expected a Navy Van."

Then the angel, who seemed a bit rough around the edges said, "Those f&$% guys won't be here till tomorrow and then they won't know where the f&$% they're going. You better stick with Joe; I'm on my way to Yokosuka. Hop in."

Joe was driving a beat-up Toyota pickup, (The first Toyota I ever saw) with boxes for the US Navy Supply Center in the back. I am sure that my young wife and Mom would not have approved, but I threw my seabag in the back and climbed in my first Toyota with Joe. Joe introduced himself as a Japanese American from Santa Barbara, California. He was a retired American Army Sergeant working as a runner for the Navy Supply Center at Yokosuka. He said he was waiting for his permanent Civil Service appointment to be approved. He said he was a shoo-in since he could speak both English and Japanese, was a veteran, and could outwork ten f&$% civil service employees. I thought but did not say, *Joe, you probably need to clean up your language.* You do not tell an angel how to talk.

Joe saved me. When we got to Yokosuka, everyone knew Joe. He told the Marine at the gate that he found a stray sailor at the airport. Joe took me to the transit barracks.

"No," I said. "I have to report to my submarine."

Joe said, "Your submarine is gone. She is doing those State Department Port Visits to make friends or some such crap."

Joe was right. My submarine was gone. A few days later, as if he had adopted me, he came by to tell me I was going to sea. They were going to put me on an LST that was taking a large Marine contingent to Okinawa and then to the Philippines. I was to be dumped off in Okinawa to catch my submarine. I thought Joe should be applying to be a spy rather than a clerk at the supply center, but then perhaps he was. I never saw Joe again. In my heart, I have always believed that Joe was my guardian angel.

First Sea Duty - LST (Landing Ship, Tank)

So, for my first real sea duty, I was crammed in with hundreds of Marines who were pumped up and looking for a battle or at least a fight. They looked at the lone sailor in their midst as an enemy. I love the Marine Corps. I'd even thought about joining the Marines, but on this LST, I was not welcomed by the Marines.

About the third day aboard the LST, I was on deck to get away from the 24 hours per day Marine Poker Game when a young Navy Ensign came up to me and asked what I was doing with a bunch of Marines. I told him my sad story.

He said, "Well how would you like to be TAD (Temporary Additional Duty) to Ship's Company? If you're a Sonarman, we can teach you to stand Radar Watches. Our Radarmen are now standing Port and Starboard watches (Six hours on and six hours off). If you can qualify, all three of you will be 4 hours on and 8 hours off and I'll give you a real bunk and a pass to use the chow hall anytime it's open."

I was saved again!

I loved standing Radar Watches and being a part of the LST Crew and I think the Marines were happy to be rid of me. I heard them calling me the Navy Spy. I am sure they never accepted that they were part of the Navy.

Between evading typhoons and numerous schedule changes, I missed my submarine again. After about six weeks on the LST, I was beginning to feel like part of the crew, and they treated me like one of them. The experience as a qualified Radar Operator served me well on my submarine.

The USS Capitaine (SS 336) was a fleet boat without a snorkel and when she needed to charge batteries or transit any distance, she went on the surface with four big sixteen-cylinder GM diesel engines. The radar system on Capitaine was much like the one on the LST and my experience gave me a leg-up in qualifying for radar watches.

FIRST SUBMARINE DUTY

I did finally catch the USS Capitaine in Okinawa and while I was welcomed on board, I did not get my bunk for almost a year. I rotated between hot bunking and skid bunking. A skid bunk was a torpedo skid. After a torpedo was fired, we would lash a flat panel to the torpedo skid, throw a mattress on it, and I would have a bunk until we reloaded torpedoes again. Hot bunking was borrowing the bunk of someone who was on watch. When you hot bunked, there was no sleeping on sheets. I took my blanket and climbed into an empty bunk, on top of the mattress cover, and prayed for sleep.

I became a Forward Torpedo Room rat. I loved being in the Forward Torpedo Room. I was told that the real sailors lived in the Forward Torpedo Room. The residents of the Forward Torpedo Room included the Torpedomen and a variety of other crew members. Some of the Forward Torpedo Room crew included my boss, *Wild Bill* Murphy, a very salty First Class Sonarman and *Gunner* Hughes, a throwback from the days when all the submarines had deck guns. Gunner had changed his rate to Sonarman to stay on submarines, but we all knew he was a Gunner's Mate at heart. Gunner and Murphy called the Torpedomen *Knuckle Draggers*, but I didn't dare. These were just a few of the old salts who lived in the Forward Torpedo Room, the roughest riding place on the boat in heavy seas. I always hot bunked in the Forward Torpedo Room.

God had blessed me by putting me on the Texas Gulf Coast for my childhood. I spent half of my life as a child at sea in small boats and I loved the rough seas. One of the old salts in the Torpedo Room called me a *Young Salt* because it was unusual for young guys to not get seasick when we were in rough seas, and there were plenty of rough seas in the Western Pacific that year. It was the season for typhoons!

TYPHOON!

Before the USS Capitaine would leave the Western Pacific, I would have my sea legs tested as never before, and while there have been a few tough seas since then, that was the roughest and toughest sea time I have seen. There was one typhoon that there was no running from. We turned our bow in the direction of the storm and spent several hours securing loose equipment. The Captain announced on the '1MC' (public address system) what to expect and the old salts let us know what was coming. It was worse than even the old salts expected.

The old fleet non-snorkel submarine had a cigarette deck and an open bridge rather than the more modern enclosed sail. During the storm, everyone had to take their regular watches or be in their bunks. Some of us volunteered for extended watches as lookouts on the bridge since we closed and dogged the conning tower hatch and we knew we would be topside for a long time. Before we hit the storm, I thought the Captain was going a bit overboard when they tied the lookouts and the Officer of the Deck together and then tied us all to the bridge. That decision saved our lives. I have seen a lot of white water, but that day, when you looked up, as high as you could see there was nothing but water breaking over the ship. The water was boiling, and it was white. It tossed our 312-foot submarine around like a toy.

After being tossed around by the seas, a major section of the bow superstructure broke loose, and for many hours, before it gave way, it pounded against the hull. These days, when I am quiet, I can hear that pounding of metal on metal and recall wondering if I would ever see my family again. I was also thanking God for letting me be part of a real sea story. I had finally experienced the excitement and danger I had been looking for since high school. While I was fearful, it was a fear that I would not be good enough to be a Submarine Sailor. I was where I belonged.

Sub Sailor Heads Home

After the storm was over and we made minimal repairs, it was clear that the USS Capitaine was well built. She was ugly with a section of the forward superstructure gone, but she was seaworthy and those big GMC's took us on a direct path to help with the onshore disaster. The Japanese folks never doubted that these Americans were their friends and I was puffed up with pride to be a part of the US Navy and the Submarine Service.

Before we left for San Diego, we patched up the forward superstructure and the Captain let the crew paint a huge shark's mouth on the bow. It looked as if the shark had its mouth open. Submariners still talk about the submarine that came into Broadway Pier, San Diego, California that December, just before Christmas, with a shark's mouth bow.

| USS Capitaine (SS-336)

I was on the #1 Bow Line coming into port. I saw my wife with our baby girl waving from the pier. They had survived being stranded alone in a big city and I had survived becoming a salty submarine sailor.

Many years later, I saw that old submarine again in Italy. She was charging her batteries. I would know the sound of those engines anywhere. The former USS Capitaine was now part of the Italian Navy. She was the Alfredo Cappellini (S 507). While she no longer had her shark's teeth, she was still training young sailors and serving her country.

This Sea Story is special to me because it is about the day I became a submarine sailor. I'm still a submarine sailor sixty-plus years later. I'm just on extended shore duty. If some SSN needs a Diving Officer for the North Atlantic where the seas are always rough, I'm available, and I would bet my pay check I would qualify quickly. I'm sure they do not need me because there are qualified volunteers from Texas and across America. These volunteers and their submarines are busy stalking threats to the United States every day. Many of these threats hide in the deep, cold oceans of the world but they will never be safe from our Submariners.

American Submariners and our Submarines are the best in the world. American shipyards continue to build the best submarines and warships in the world.

RECIPES

BEACH FISH CHOWDER

30 - 45 Minutes
Serves 4 to 6

Ingredients

- 6 Large Potatoes, Cut into Chunks
- 3 Large Onions, Quartered
- 1 Pound Seafood, Usually Fresh Fish
- 2 Cans Evaporated Milk (Substitute Fresh Milk if Available)
- Salt & Pepper
- 3 Large Carrots, Cut into Chunks
- Cooked Bacon Including the Drippings
- 3 Stalks Celery, Cut into Chunks

Note: Carrots and Celery Are Very Good, But Any Other Fresh Vegetable Like Fresh Squash Is Also Good

Directions

1. Boil Potatoes In 2 Quarts of Water Until Fork Done, and then Lower Heat to Simmer.
2. Add Onions, Carrots, Celery, and Cook Approximately 15 Minutes.
3. Add Seafood, Usually Fish Fillets
4. Add Bacon and Or Drippings
5. Add Milk
6. Season with Salt and Pepper
7. Simmer for About 15 Minutes After Seafood Is Added
8. Adjust the Thickness of Broth by Adding More Water

IRON SKILLET FRIED POTATOES

30 minutes
Serves 6 or More
Side Dish for Breakfast or Fried Fish

Ingredients

- 4 Slices Bacon
- 3 Onions, Thin Sliced or Chopped
- 6 Medium Potatoes, Sliced or Medium Size Chunks
- 2-3 Tablespoons Bacon Drippings (Substitute Lard or Oil)
- Salt & Pepper

Directions

1. Sauté Bacon Over Medium Heat in A Large Iron Skillet
2. Add Additional Drippings or Oil as Needed
3. Cook Onions Until Clear and Tender
4. Add Potatoes
5. Lightly Toss Until Potatoes Are Lightly Coated with Bacon Drippings or Oil
6. Cover the Skillet and Cook Until Potatoes Are Fork Tender, (About 15 Min. Depending on Thickness of Potato).
7. Remove Skillet Cover – Increase Temperature to About Medium High
8. Dry Fry Potatoes Until Desired Shade of Brown Is Reached (Turn as Needed to Evenly Fry)
9. Season Using Salt and Pepper as Needed

IRON SKILLET PAN-FRIED FLOUNDER

5 Minutes per Fish

Ingredients

- 1 Whole Small Flounder
- 2-4 Tablespoons Crisco (For Small Skillet)
- Salt and Pepper
- ½ Cup Flour (For Dusting/Optional)

Directions

1. Clean Fresh Flounder and pack on Ice
2. Dry Flounder When Ready to Cook
3. Salt and Pepper Flounder on Both Sides
4. Dust Flounder with Flour or Fry Dry
5. Pre Heat Iron Skillet
6. Add Just Enough Crisco to Cover Skillet Bottom
7. Add Flounder and Fry on each side until Crusty (No more than 2-3 min)
8. Remove Flounder and Serve with Skillet Fries

Note: If Cooking Several Flounder, Just Add Crisco as Needed for Each Flounder and Repeat Process.

GRANNY'S FRIED MASHED POTATO SANDWICHES

Ingredients

- Bacon Grease
- Medium Onion, Chopped
- Leftover Mashed Potatoes
- Sliced Bread, 2 Slices for each Sandwich

Directions

1. Melt One Tablespoon of Bacon Grease in Cast Iron Skillet Over Medium Low Heat
2. Add Onions to the Bacon Grease and Cook Until Soft
3. Add 2 Cups of Leftover Mashed Potatoes to the Onions
4. Mix Well
5. Spread Warm Onion & Mashed Potato Mixture to Slice of Bread
6. Add Second Slice of Bread
7. Enjoy!

ACKNOWLEDGMENTS

I am thankful for my parents, grandparents, aunts, uncles, teachers, and coaches. They raised me and educated me. They are my heroes. They told me to go play. PW Morrow (Grandad) said life is a game, learn how to play it. They knew that playing with cousins, playing on the playgrounds, and playing in organized sports and school activities was a valuable part of preparing for life.

Thanks to the parents, coaches, teachers, and kids at Georgetown High School in Georgetown Texas, and the members of the Sun City Eagle Booster Club. You have convinced me that the concept of kids and play is alive and well in 2020. The kids the Eagle Boosters support know how to play. They give their all every game. They know how to be a part of a team; they know how to win and when they lose they do it with grace. They will be good at the game of life.

With my retirement to Georgetown in 2004 and a golf score of 120 on a good day, I decided to go back to the only game that I was good at, Work. I shared my plan with Temple Pouncey, a sportswriter, and fellow Eagle Booster. Temple said "Come with me to the Senior University class on Memoir Writing, it will be fun, and we can share our life stories." It was fun and I discovered that I had lived a life worth remembering.

Temple returned to the Dallas area, but before he left, I joined him in a memoir writing group that has sustained me with friendship, expertise in medicine, genealogy, art, flying helicopters, and surviving major life challenges. I would not have written any part of my life story without Temple Pouncey, Pat Clendenin, Linda Clark, Kim Hovanky, Walt Henderson, Kathy Henderson, Jo Bryan, Jay Pierson, and the Senior University memoir writing instructors, Alan Dawes, Sid Frost, Jackie Switzer and Karen Hett. Thanks, Guys!

Over the years, I filled a closet with handwritten stories in spiral notebooks that I shared with my wife and my memoir group. I did not share the stories or the characters in the stories with anyone else. Two years ago, as an alternative Christmas present, I wrote stories to my children from their Great Grandfathers. The letters were based on my memory, my research, and the stories I wrote about two real American men I worshiped as a kid. The letters were well received and the idea of sharing my early life with my family and friends began to take shape.

Windmills to Submarines is a family project. It would not exist without the help of my wife, Jerrie, and my daughters, Madonna and Sarah. My wife took the kid stories from my notebooks and converted them to Word documents that were used as the basis of this book. I transitioned these stories into my early life as my family navigated through World War II and four moves in South Texas. While my earliest memory is playing in Granny's chicken coop, the first really exciting adventure as a kid was climbing Grandad's Windmill. It was worth the risk of a switching and falling to an early death to climb that windmill. My first submarine duty was my first really exciting adventure as an adult. Submarine duty was worth any risk. I was no longer a kid.

My daughter Madonna, a computer genius and a creative thinker and my daughter Sarah, a nurse, artist, writer, and amateur genealogist combined to edit and create the kid story *Windmills to Submarines* that I now share with the rest of the family and perhaps friends. Thank you, Jerrie, Madonna, and Sarah. Working with you has been the highlight of this project.

I gave an early rough draft of Windmills to Submarines to my friend Dr. Kim Thinh Hovanky. Kim is the author, with her brother

Louis, of, THE NOBILITY OF OUR HEARTS FROM BEN SUC TO SAI GON TO AUSTIN. Their book is an epic story of a Vietnamese American Family. Kim's book is a Masterpiece. I hoped Kim would give me an idea of what I should do next. She did. With Kim's input and my desire to make sure that the folks that raised me were never forgotten, I decided the book should be completed and published. Thank you, Kim, for your continued input and your friendship.

Writing treasured memories of a life worth living is a joy. Going through the process of preparing those memories for publication is a chore. I was tempted to just send the latest draft to the family with a note to enjoy, or just stick the draft in the file cabinet. Then I rememberd the example set by my friend R.G. Andersen-Wyckoff. When R.G. has an idea, he writes a book and completes the project. When he wrote and published the insightful book, THE SECRET OF PFADLER'S MOUNTAIN, it should have prepared us to accept the precarious nature of everyday life before the pandemic of 2020. Thanks, R.G., for being a great role model and for being willing to assist me.

This book would not have been completed and would not have been published without the mentoring and creativity of Victoria Twead at Ant Press.

Dick Witte

ABOUT THE AUTHOR

Richard (Dick Witte) is the author of *Windmills to Submarines*, a memoir of being a kid in South Texas small towns from the end of the Great Depression and the beginning of World War II, to the near end of the 1950s.

Dick was raised and educated by small town, hardworking heroes. He has experienced a life worth living.

Dick is a retired college professor/professor emeritus. He is also a retired US Navy submarine sailor.

After being expelled from kindergarten, Dick received an excellent education at Saint Michael's Catholic School in Cuero, Texas, Saint Joseph's Catholic School in Beeville, Texas, and the public schools in Ingleside, Texas.

After high school, Dick was trained in electronics, sonar, and submarines by the Navy. Dick retired from the Navy as the Squadron Combat Systems Officer for Sonar in a squadron of nuclear fast attack submarines.

Highlights of his Navy career included taking five nuclear submarines on their first sea trials, and initial dives, in the company of the legendary Admiral Hyman Rickover.

Dick's favorite assignment, while in the Navy, was as Chief of the Boat on the submarine that eventually became the most decorated ship in Navy History. The most prized award in his career was a simple compliment. Admiral Rickover told Dick's captain, "You probably ought to keep that diving officer." The Admiral didn't give many compliments.

After many extended cold war submarine patrols, Dick was awarded a Navy college scholarship. Dick loved college and eventually received a Ph.D. from Old Dominion University in Virginia. He also completed several post-graduate special programs including Developmental Education Certification at Appalachian State University and the Higher Education Leadership Program at The Wharton School.

Dick served in multiple roles in Higher Education including counselor and classroom teacher. He taught students from college freshman to doctoral candidates, and he learned much from his students. Dick held administrative positions as Coordinator of Admissions and Records, Dean of Students, and Vice President for Student and Enrollment Services at Tidewater Community College.

Dick loved his work in the Navy and Higher Education.

Dick's favorite volunteer work was serving for many years as a volunteer adult literacy tutor.

Contact Dick by email: dickwitte20@gmail.com

Dick in the chicken coop kindly colorized by Ken Ferguson

THE SILENT SERVICE HAS THE WATCH

If you enjoyed this Sea Story, stay tuned for more remembered Sea Stories in my Memoir, 'Sub Sailor' that follows a Texas Kid from Mess Cook to Chief of the Boat to Master Chief and Submarine Squadron Combat Systems Officer for Sonar.

Shark's mouth submarine kindly colorized by Ken Ferguson